The Company and the Activist

Addressing the rise of a new breed of activists who present a real threat not only to reputations but to business operations, this book explores what businesses need to understand about these communities, why they should be taken seriously, and how business leaders can successfully navigate this shifting terrain.

Existing business books address only the communications challenges involved in the rise of these new communities, but this book goes beyond PR issues to the very real impact on business decisions – and acknowledges that businesses must understand activists, and vice versa, if progress is to be made. To lead this conversation, the book includes interviews and contributions from key players across activism and businesses to look at how both sides operate and what success looks like for them. It also features practical steps that businesses can take to build a network of supporters, drawing on global examples from the corporate sector, grassroots campaigns, and people and organisations taking up the mantle of activism.

Leaders and professionals working in all aspects of business, across industries and firm types, will appreciate learning about what drives activists and how businesses can work with them to not only avoid reputational damage, but to create stronger connections and, perhaps, a better world.

Stuart Thomson is a public affairs and communications specialist, and published author. He advises clients on all elements of their political engagement and reputation management running his own consultancy, CWE Communications. Stuart regularly provides comment across the media, is an honorary research fellow at the University of Aberdeen, a regular speaker at conferences and delivers training for leadership teams. He was listed as one of the Top 100 Public Affairs Consultants by Total Politics, was shortlisted for the IoD and CIPR Director of the Year award, and won Vuelio online influencer of the year in the current affairs category.

The Company and the Activist

Going Beyond PR

Stuart Thomson

Routledge
Taylor & Francis Group

NEW YORK AND LONDON

Designed cover image: Getty

First published 2025
by Routledge
605 Third Avenue, New York, NY 10158

and by Routledge
4 Park Square, Milton Park, Abingdon, Oxon OX14 4RN

Routledge is an imprint of the Taylor & Francis Group, an informa business

© 2025 Stuart Thomson

The right of Stuart Thomson to be identified as author of this work has been asserted in accordance with sections 77 and 78 of the Copyright, Designs and Patents Act 1988.

Library of Congress Cataloging-in-Publication Data
Names: Thomson, Stuart, 1972– author.
Title: The company and the activist : going beyond PR / Stuart Thomson.
Description: New York, NY : Routledge, 2025. | Includes bibliographical references and index. |
Identifiers: LCCN 2024027892 (print) | LCCN 2024027893 (ebook) | ISBN 9781032444000 (hardback) | ISBN 9781032443843 (paperback) | ISBN 9781003371908 (ebook)
Subjects: LCSH: Corporate image–Social aspects. | Public relations–Social aspects. | Social responsibility of business. | Community activists. | Protest movements.
Classification: LCC HD59.2 .T459 2025 (print) | LCC HD59.2 (ebook) | DDC 658.2–dc23/eng/20240719
LC record available at https://lccn.loc.gov/2024027892
LC ebook record available at https://lccn.loc.gov/2024027893

ISBN: 978-1-032-44400-0 (hbk)
ISBN: 978-1-032-44384-3 (pbk)
ISBN: 978-1-003-37190-8 (ebk)

DOI: 10.4324/9781003371908

Typeset in Sabon
by Taylor & Francis Books

This book is dedicated to my long-suffering family – Alex, Will, Callum, Elenya, Mum, Dad, and Iain

Contents

Illustrations

Preface

As someone who has always been interested in politics and current affairs, the role that activists play has always seemed central to delivering change. Whether that is driving change by government or, increasingly, in companies, activists seem to play a valuable and interesting role.

But whilst activists always appear willing to reflect on what they do and how they do it, companies have seemed less interested in learning. An adversarial approach dominated by a 'business knows best' view of the world has led some companies, and executives, to a very dark place. Added to that, the tide seems to be turning. Younger people are more interested in what makes a company tick and how they deliver their operations.

That has led me to write this book. I wanted to try and break down some of the misunderstandings and misperceptions. Maybe to see whether that person who first became interested in politics and current affairs by watching John Craven's Newsround on BBC was right to think that activists play a critical role in change. As with my previous books, I wanted the discussion to be interesting, informative and practical for all those who read it.

To be honest, this book has taken me a little longer to write than was originally anticipated. This is largely down to having to look for work as a newly established freelancer. Running my own business was not something I had thought of when I started writing this book. But circumstances change...

Even more so than ever, that means the support provided by my family has been so important to me. Alex, Will, Callum and Elenya have been encouraging me at every step both with this book and in getting CWE Communications off the ground. My mum, dad and brother (Maureen, Bill, and Iain) have also been very keen for me to get this book over the line!

I have been fortunate that many people have contributed their thoughts to this book which has helped in the aim of bringing new and interesting insights, as well as making it practical. I firmly believe that hearing from a range of voices makes a book of this type more enjoyable to read. As with my previous book for Routledge, Reputation in Business, these contributions mean that I do not have to pretend to have expert insight into every aspect of this complex and challenging issue. Together the voices bring unique perspectives from which conclusions can be drawn. A huge thank you for all their time and effort go to Jon Alexander, Lucy von Sturmer, Scott Goodstein, Tom McGarry, Paul Gerrard, Robert Blood, Michael Tunks, Tessa Wernink, Dr Lynn Bennie, Brian Ross (Stansted Airport Watch), Janneke Parrish, McKenzie Ursch, Sarah Waddington CBE, Helen Fry and Graham Olver.

Thank you also to Matthew Smith. Matthew always instinctively knows how I should approach a challenge and helps to shape my ideas. Working with him over the years (this isn't our first project!) has been a privilege. I have enjoyed working again with Meredith Norwich and the team, including Bethany Nelson, at Routledge. Working together we make a great team!

As always with my books, faults and failings remain my own and I would be delighted to receive feedback from everyone who reads this.

Thank you all.
Stuart Thomson
April 2024, www.stuartthomson.co.uk

Introduction

Businesses face challenges from many audiences. They are constantly balancing the needs and requirements of those audiences. The impact that some have can be greater than others. They often impact on the operations, returns or reputation of the business and, as a result, are taken seriously. Businesses have teams and advisers in place to help them manage these audiences.

But we are witnessing the rise of a new breed of activists who offer a real threat not just to reputations but to an ever-wider range of business operations as well. As a result, they need to be taken seriously. The activists represent key parts of a business's operations. They cannot be compartmentalised as many may have been in the past. As John Harrington, UK Editor of *PR Week* said in the Beyond the Noise Podcast:

> We are going to see a lot more activism. This has been one of the big themes that has been changing the communications industry… with social media having fuelled this sense of investor activism, social change activism and employee activism. That is where this industry becomes incredibly important to clients. There is an opportunity there but also a lot of threats.

The communities that these activist groups represent vary but they are always motivated and dedicated. Their impact can be substantial but there are different ways in which companies can react. Some reactions work more effectively than others. Some are more constructive than others.

Alongside this, there is also a more recent drive towards companies themselves being socially motivated. 'Activist' companies are on the rise. They can have similar aims to community activists and may choose to work alongside them.

Other businesses, unfortunately, try to disguise their actions through 'washing'. They appear to choose to continue established practices as opposed to taking the difficult decisions needed to, for instance, protect the planet or their workforce. They wish to present a view of themselves to the outside world which is, at best, misleading. This shows PR leading business actions and activity. A potential short-term fix that does nothing to address underlying issues or concerns, especially those expressed by activists.

DOI: 10.4324/9781003371908-1

It is not just businesses either, some governments involve themselves in 'washing' to disguise or distract from their poor behaviour which is out of step with expectations of those they wish to trade with or attract investment from.

The setting

There is surprisingly little written about the interplay between activists and businesses. This practical book is an attempt to address this deficiency.

In the first place, a lack of clarity over what an activist really is because the range of activity is so wide appears to be growing as activists seek more opportunities to push their agendas. But from the perspective of many businesses, this can mean there is a lack of clarity over who has ultimate responsibility for dealing with activists. It has largely depended on the type of activist action being faced – corporate communications, legal, marketing etc. But that means action can be faced for some period of time before being escalated or placed in a wider effort by the business. In other words, it can be compartmentalised and not dealt with at a senior level. This can lead to greater levels of frustration, motivating activists still further.

As Brayden King explains, collective action against corporates can be effective.[1] He points to their ability to shine a light on behaviours and the ramifications that can have. In a study in which he was involved that found 'on average, a 1 percent drop in stock price within a 26-day period of a protest targeting that company'.[2]

Of course, the actions undertaken by activists vary and are designed to raise the profile of the company's behaviour often to bring it to the attention of as many people as possible. Media coverage, according to the same study, was a key factor in the effectiveness of the action. They did, however, appreciate that 'companies that had received a lot of coverage prior to a protest did not see as big of a decline'.[3]

This highlights the critical role that reputation management plays. Put simply, invest in creating a good reputation and then an activist attack will potentially have less impact. Audiences already know and understand an organisation and that can bring some protection. They will have built resistance in advance of requiring it. For King:

> I think that activists increasingly do have a place at the table... We see them as voices that matter, and companies and governments throughout the world are increasingly willing to let them in and have them help set better practices.

From this perspective, activists are important in maintaining accountability and holding businesses to account. The activists could be highlighting illegal activities. They could be highlighting a divergence between what a company says and actually does. Or they could be trying to move the conversation on to change behaviour. When, for instance, the Church of England came under pressure from activists over their investment portfolio, the Church itself had already called on fossil fuel companies to do more to tackle climate change but had retained investments in those same companies. This made it ripe for activist scrutiny. Most recently, the Church of England has excluded all fossil fuel companies from an endowment fund.

Other activists may try to change behaviour and attitudes. This can take a long time but then enables others to scrutinise companies for not adhering to those new societal expectations. Just consider the way in which links with the slave trade have been highlighted and the way in which companies and institutions have had to apologise, remove statues and appreciate how they benefitted in the past from the slave trade.

There needs to be a level of understanding on the part of activists and businesses. It demonstrates that at their heart both 'sides' have to consider their communication (see Table I.1).

Businesses have to focus on the fact there is no one type of activist group. No one form of action any of them could take. As we will consider, they keep innovating. The most effective activist groups are those that keep ahead of the organisations they are challenging. Bringing communication and actions designed to highlight an organisation's failures is the job of the activist. They use the spotlight to secure behaviour change. This is fundamentally about knowledge.

On the flipside the most effective businesses are those that keep ahead of activist action. It could be argued that those are the ones that do not require any action by activists. But there is also an element of 'tall poppy syndrome'. Activists need to tackle the large companies, those with a high profile, those led by executives who are not afraid of the media or political spotlight. If activists can force them to change their behaviour or adopt a leading approach, then others will follow. It becomes the market norm.

Table I.1 Strategies

Activists	Businesses
Campaigns are well informed	Challenge and rebut campaign
Set out an agenda of standards, behaviours and practices	Set out an agenda of standards, behaviours and practices
Identify gaps in a businesses' agenda	Address gaps in the agenda
Capable of generating media interest	Improve knowledge in advance of activist campaign
Maintain interest in the issue over time	Take action / distract
Engage with wider range of stakeholders	Engage with wider range of stakeholders

Much of the recent discussion has been given to the rise of activist companies and activist CEOs. These push their competitors, suppliers, others in the industry and stakeholders to adopt higher standards of behaviour. Some push this into the political sphere as well and are not afraid to push governments as well. In some instances, they end up in open conflict with political audiences.

An activist CEO or company can push their agenda by implementing new policies, pushing for social or environmental reforms, and advocating for change on a broader scale. More sceptical audiences may believe that they do this to gain a market advantage, especially when younger consumers are often considered to want this from the companies they do business with. It can also help a company to attract and retain top talent as many employees want to work for companies who take their social and environmental commitments seriously.

Activism, on the part of a business, can help build a positive reputation which establishes strong relationships with customers, investors, and other stakeholders. This can lead to increased brand loyalty, customer satisfaction and financial success. The personal motivation of the CEO should not be discounted either.

There is no doubting the commitment of many who continue along their chosen path even if it brings critical media or political reaction.

Some of the world's most high-profile companies are considered to have activist CEOs:

- Tim Cook of Apple, who has been a vocal advocate for privacy and environmental protections.
- Satya Nadella of Microsoft, who has pushed for diversity and inclusion within the tech industry.
- Howard Schultz of Starbucks, who has been a leader in the movement to provide healthcare and education benefits to workers.

As we will see this does not make any of these companies perfect and they are far from immune to the attention of activists.

But if we flip this conversation around, we can consider that it would be a brave organisation that does not take these issues seriously, especially when the competition for sales or employees is fierce.

Looking at the role of new activist CEOs, Aaron K. Chatterji and Michael W. Toffel believe that the CEOs need to ask themselves a series of questions:

- What to weigh in on.
- Where to weigh in.
- How to weigh in.[4]

An activist CEO also needs, they suggest, to align their internal stakeholders and predict the reaction and gauge the results.[5]

These again demonstrate the critical role of communication but also the management of risk.

But there is also, according to several studies, a realisation that consumers and employees want to deal with businesses that take their social responsibilities more seriously. There is also a trickle-down effect throughout a supply chain. If a business insists on certain standards of behaviour and practice, then this has to happen throughout the supply chain. This, in turn, shifts expectations for all of us over time.

Activist attacks can have a range of downsides for any organisation. These include:

- Reputational damage – campaigns can harm an organisation's reputation, causing customers and stakeholders to question the company's ethics and values and whether to continue to do business with it.
- Financial impact – campaigns can lead to a decline in share price, which can have a significant financial impact on the company, its shareholders and even its viability.
- Legal liabilities – activists may often adopt a legal approach, which can result in costly legal battles, damaging fines or penalties, and have personal and professional implications.
- Distracting from 'business as usual' – an attack can divert significant resources and attention which can take away from the focus on core operations.
- Employee morale – attacks can have a negative impact on employee morale.

The rise of activists

Activists are nothing new. Groups have long put pressure on businesses and governments to behave in certain ways or pass new laws to offer protection. It is argued by some that nothing really happens without such pressure being applied.

Activism appears to vary over time. This could be down to social, economic or political factors and, of course, a changing legal setting.

But in recent years we have witnessed:

- The power of social media and how it can be used to facilitate and build support for causes and campaigns.
- The increasing profile of Net Zero and environmental concerns and a spotlight being placed on companies.
- Labour rights – these vary across countries, but workers still come together to force change.
- Ethical behaviour – whether it be the protection of human rights, attempts to improve diversity and inclusion or a number of other matters, these issues are being pushed by many.
- Shareholder activism – and the use of legal tools to facilitate and force change.

- Consumer activism – consumers remain keen to undertake boycotts and other measures to impact on business operations.
- Lobbying – many activists understand that a great deal can be achieved by governments passing new laws and regulations.

What activists have become ever more aware of, and adept at, is working through media channels – online and traditional. They are fully aware of the need to draw attention to their actions and the value that can bring. That has been accompanied by a more diverse and diffuse media and demands that feed off each other.

But other forms of action include:

- Civil disobedience – normally non-violent actions such as blocking or slowing traffic.
- Direct action – occupying a building or daubing paint across a HQ building.
- Local community action – focused on particular sites or challenges, rather than nationally.
- Education and awareness-raising – working, sometimes in a quieter way, to promote a course of action.
- Working together – with a focus on coalition-building to increase their impact and strength of voice.

How do they decide on which type of action is most appropriate and effective? This should come down to some of the basics of good communication. Sometimes a campaign may call for loud, public actions; other campaigns need to be built more quietly, over time with audiences that can really make a difference. Just as with any communications campaign, the tactics can vary over time while learning which are the most effective.

The activists consider:

- The aims and objectives of the campaign.
- The intended target of the campaign.
- The resources available to them; people as well as financial.
- How to maximise the value-for-money that they can deliver.
- The risks involved.
- How the campaign will contribute towards gaining support.
- The timescales involved and the prospects of success.

When it comes to the risk analysis, activists will reflect upon the reaction that the campaign could elicit but there are often considerations such as the legal implications for any individuals involved in action. An arrest for breaking the law may be unfortunate but deliver additional profile that the campaign could then capitalise on. But the individuals involved need to know what the possible consequences are before action is taken.

Activists will often focus on building momentum. The more they can encourage others to take action, the further the pressure will spread. Successful action can lead to more engagement and support.

Activist campaigns can ebb and flow over time. A report by the Social Change Lab[6] reinforced some popular findings about what makes a protest movement successful such as the importance of non-violence and the idea that numbers matter, the value of people power. But it also suggested that timing, external factors and luck can all play a role as well. That means all those involved have to be constantly vigilant, opportunistic, aware and react when necessary. Proactivity on all sides appears to have a key role.

The activist community itself challenge their own approaches. The excellent book by Jon Alexander, *Citizens: Why the Key to Fixing Everything Is All of Us*, suggests that we all have a role to play in securing change:

> By embracing, enacting, and fortifying the Citizen Story, we will be able to face the challenges of economic insecurity, climate crisis, public health threats, and political polarisation, together. We will be able to build a future together.[7]

Some activists see effectiveness in being oppositional, for others there needs to be a coming together. This means the 'modern activist' needs to be an expert in action, communication and the law, and be able to develop constructive relationships with those they may have a fundamental problem with.

The reality is that there is no single form of activism or activist. They all vary depending on the target, the aim and the tactics employed.

Possibly by accident, Elon Musk proved the power of activists when he blamed them for the fall-off in revenue of Twitter (as it was then).[8] A number of advertisers suspended their spend with the platform which led him to tweet:

> Twitter has had a massive drop in revenue, due to activist groups pressuring advertisers, even though nothing has changed with content moderation, and we did everything we could to appease the activists. Extremely messed up! They're trying to destroy free speech in America.[9]

When one of the richest and most successful businesspeople in the world is impacted by activist intervention and openly recognises it then the action is having an impact.

This book brings the issues involved in the relationship between activists and businesses to life through the use of interviews and contributions from key players across community groups and businesses. The book will look at how both sides operate and what success looks like for them.

The book will also include practical steps that can be taken to build relationships and understanding on all parts.

Examples will be drawn from across the corporate sector, where employees come together to challenge decisions (particularly in the tech sector); grassroots community campaigns (including those against infrastructure projects such as airport expansion); and those taking a more 'societal' view about damage to the environment or improved provision for deprived communities.

Many business books have so far failed to look at the issues involved in the rise of new activist communities in any detail. Instead, the existing literature considers only the communications challenges involved or considers activists in distinct compartments, such as shareholder activists.

This book will consider the issues in the context of business decisions, risk management and reputation management, bringing a new challenging perspective. If neither side takes the time to learn about and understand the other then progress will never be made.

Some companies may always choose to ignore social issues for a variety of reasons. Some may simply consider maximising profits to be the prime aim; others may believe that social issues are a distraction from their core activities; others may prefer that competitors take on the mantle and the potentially higher profile that comes with that.

In other cases, an organisation may be unaware of the issues they face, lack the experience or expertise to recognise or deal with them, or may believe that the issue has already been addressed.

In many of these circumstances, activists play a positive role in helping the organisation address the problems they face. Without the attention of activists, the problem could continue unaddressed. This may not help the company, community or wider society.

But there are also examples of organisations, particularly businesses, that claim a certain standard of behaviour but then fail to adhere to that. This could be deliberate or could be by accident.

Some organisations go still further and try and 'wash' their reputations. This is another issue that the book will reflect upon.

Impressions

For many people, the impression they have of activists has traditionally been one of disruption which inflicts damage. The type of damage varies between financial, reputational and physical.

What is clear is that direct action of the type often associated with more high-profile activity, such as that carried out by Extinction Rebellion, is typically unpopular with the public. Violent action is similarly frowned upon.

But if the action raises the profile of an issue, could that be considered a 'win' for the activist group?

Polling provided by YouGov demonstrates this very well when it comes to Extinction Rebellion. According to them:[10]

- Fame (have heard of): 69%.
- Popularity (liked by): 21%.
- Disliked (by): 32%.
- Neutral: 16%.

They also found that the group's popularity was highest amongst Millennials.

Another direct-action campaign that secured attention was undertaken by Insulate Britain. They spent several weeks blocking motorway junctions to highlight climate change and pushing the government to make homes more energy efficient. Their actions brought them into conflict with the general public and the police. According to polls this led to an increase in opposition to the group's actions.[11] Things got so bad that the UK Government felt compelled to take action and so introduced the Public Order Bill. The legislation was, however, seen by many to be an attack on the right to protest.

> Through the raft of new protest-specific offences, expansion of police powers and introduction of 'protest banning orders', the Public Order Bill stands to create a significant chilling effect on our ability to stand up to power, dissuading people from exercising their right to protest and to freedom of assembly as well as sweeping more and more people into the criminal justice system for doing so.[12]

What next?

This book looks to explore the relationships between businesses and activists and look at different types of examples. As in my previous books, the approach is to be as practical as possible. Rather than focusing too much on the theories, the book focuses on what businesses and activists do, how they behave and what lessons can be drawn for all those involved.

The book will:

- examine the rise of the new activists, exploring their nature and providing examples of campaigns
- consider the rise of community-wide campaigns, their key campaigning tools and what makes them tick
- detail the combination of strategies used
- look at the types of communities that come together to campaign such as employees, shareholders and community groups
- consider how business should think about community action in the context of the growing ESG movement
- demonstrate that the campaigns range from the local to the global, often joining up with each other to maximise the power of their impact on businesses
- help businesses avoid the pitfalls of community engagement.

Failing to take any form of community action seriously risks business operations, reputations, projects and profits.

We will also hear throughout the book from a range of experts, each of whom brings their insight to the issues involved. The contributions they make really help with my aim of making the book as practical as possible.

As will become clear in the book, there is much for all those involved to learn and without action the relationship can easily slip into one of mistrust and confrontation. Everyone has a role to play in making the relationships work.

Businesses need to think more about partnerships rather than confrontation and should not wait to be forced into action. The damage inflicted only increases if they wait until the last minute.

Each chapter of the book will consider a different aspect of the relationship between activists and companies.

It is important that we remember that activists are not always right, just as much as not all businesses are purely motivated by profit.

Helping businesses recognise the power of new activist communities is a vital first step. Each recognising the role and power of the other means they can work together to deliver on their respective aims.

This book hopes to improve those working relationships through an improved understanding of motivations, constraints and pressures.

Notes

1 Brayden King, 'Why companies should engage with activists', Kellogg Insight, 28 April 2021, https://insight.kellogg.northwestern.edu/article/why-companies-should-engage-with-activists

2 Brayden King, 'Why companies should engage with activists', Kellogg Insight, 28 April 2021, https://insight.kellogg.northwestern.edu/article/why-companies-should-engage-with-activists

3 Brayden King, 'Why companies should engage with activists', Kellogg Insight, 28 April 2021, https://insight.kellogg.northwestern.edu/article/why-companies-should-engage-with-activists

4 Aaron K. Chatterji and Michael W. Toffel. 'The new CEO activists: A playbook for polarized political times', *Harvard Business Review Magazine*, January–February 2018

5 Aaron K. Chatterji and Michael W. Toffel. 'The new CEO activists: A playbook for polarized political times', *Harvard Business Review Magazine*, January–February 2018

6 Social Change Lab, 'What makes a protest movement successful', 26 January 2023, www.socialchangelab.org/post/what-makes-a-protest-movement-successful

7 See www.jonalexander.net/the-idea

8 See Tom Espiner, 'Twitter: Elon Musk blames "activist groups" for earnings drop', *BBC*, 4 November 2022, www.bbc.co.uk/news/business-63521713

9 Elon Musk, Twitter, 4 November 2022, https://twitter.com/elonmusk/status/1588538640401018880

10 YouGov, *Extinction Rebellion*, https://yougov.co.uk/topics/politics/explore/not-for-profit/Extinction_Rebellion as at 14 December 2022

11 Jemma Connor, 'Three weeks into motorway climate change protests, public opposition has only grown', YouGov, 8 October 2021, https://yougov.co.uk/topics/poli
tics/articles-reports/2021/10/08/three-weeks-motorway-climate-change-protests-publi
12 Fair Trails, 'UK: The Public Order Bill is an attack on the right to protest', 18
October 2022, www.fairtrials.org/articles/news/uk-the-public-order-bill-is-an-atta
ck-on-the-right-to-protest/

Chapter 1

Activism

What to expect

The format of activist campaigns varies enormously. One of the hallmarks of activist activity in recent years has been the rise in the level of creativity. The tactics employed have more variety and are often better able to capture the attention of their intended audience.

There seems little doubt that the general public has become more of a target for action as well, particularly for environmental campaigners who appear to believe that more drastic action is needed to help protect the planet.

The older, more established activist actions of sit-ins, boycotts etc. have been joined by concerted efforts looking to make the most of existing levers of power. The continued rise of shareholder activism, the use of legal challenges and the creation of trade unions in tech firms, for example, all use powers already on the statute book to force change.

In other campaigns, it appears that there is an 'arms race' of activity constantly attempting to keep ahead of their intended audience and, crucially, maintain interest particularly through the media. It is often claimed there is 'no such thing as bad publicity' and in the case of activist activity that appears to be true. Even if the media coverage is negative, it serves as a constant reminder that there is a problem to be solved.

Activists actually use a variety of methods. They are not one-trick ponies.

This chapter examines the types of campaigns and attacks made on organisations. These include more traditional boycotts, petitions and strikes, as well as newer social media and media attacks, use of the law and the power of influencers / celebrities.

These can be categorised as 'insider' and 'outsider' attacks, from within the organisation or from an external audience. Both need to be considered and engaged.

What works?

In an extensive literature review, The Social Change Lab considered the success factors behind protest movements. As they identified, whilst there is research that looks at the outcomes of protest movements, there is

DOI: 10.4324/9781003371908-2

comparatively less on how protest movements can create societal change. They also acknowledge that there are significant limitations around existing research. However, that makes their review of particular interest.

Summarising their findings they found that:[1]

- There is strong evidence that non-violent protest is generally preferable to violent protest for achieving desired outcomes – pointing to evidence that non-violent protestors are more likely to persuade the public.
- There is moderate evidence that the protestors are more likely to succeed if the number of protestors is high – although the evidence on this is mixed.
- There is only limited evidence that unity of protester message and protest frequency are associated with an increased chance of protest success – although this is mainly because of a lack of research.
- It is likely that a non-violent radical flank will increase an overall movement's likelihood of achieving policy wins – with violence adversely impacting on support.
- Factors that influence the public are slightly different to those that influence policymakers – they suggest that the public are concerned with the worthiness of protesters, whereas policymakers are more influenced by the numbers of protesters and the diversity of the groups present.
- The political context is also very relevant – with success for a campaign more likely if they are highlighting an issue on which the public is already on their side; if they are exerting pressure at the start of the legislative process rather than the end; and they focus on issues recently covered in the media.
- The political context might be important enough to dominate over factors within the movement's control – despite of how well the campaign is executed.

The evidence is unclear on a number of issues related to protest movements but the review brings into sharp focus the nature of variable factors facing any campaign. There is no one single ideal model of a campaign and that has implications for both the campaign and those being campaigned against.

It also highlights the problem of time as well. It is clear that the attitudes change over time. The types of measures against smoking, fossils fuels or to protect the environment show what was unacceptable at one point in time can become acceptable later, and vice versa. The political climate changes as the electorate shifts its position.

This is often caused by a mix of new technologies and reduced costs but evidence and research, combined with campaigns, all have an impact as well. A campaign may not, therefore, deliver results immediately but can, over time, shift positions and result in action.

Challenges to activists

At the outset, any campaign has to consider what type of activity is going to work for their cause. The basics of any campaign are the same whoever is leading it. In the activist field, the driver of action may be a number of individuals motivated by securing change on an issue. But drivers will exist for companies, charities and other organisations as well.

It is not as simple as saying that activists believe in their issue more deeply or are more motivated to take action than others but that could well be the case, especially for those who kick off the whole campaign. But is an activist any more motivated than the founder of a new company? There may be a fierce argument to be had about that.

The findings of the Social Change Lab report help to illustrate the types of challenges that a campaign will face:

- How to raise its profile – impacting on the types of action to undertake.
- Motivation – how to get numbers of people involved.
- Lack of unity – there is no such thing as a unified movement, that disguises the range of opinions, actions etc.
- Worthiness does not simply exist – it is at least partly created by communication as well and it is built over time.
- Voters – any campaign needs to think about the politics involved and the reaction of voters. Motivating a small number of potential voters in an area could be more important than large national numbers. That could mean that they are completely homogenous but important electorally. There is no detaching politics from campaigning.
- Opponents to the campaign will campaign as well – there are few issues that enjoy universal support and if they did, would the issue really need to be campaigned on?

A campaign needs to consider what change it is attempting to secure, building its strategy from that point. That means being able to know:

- who their audiences are
- what their timetables are
- how to communicate with them.

In its publication, *The Case for Campaigning*, the communications consultancy Pagefield included the following in its campaigning list:[2]

- launching / signing petitions
- protests / marches
- using social media including blogs and videos

- creating stories / being interviewed in the press / on TV (often based on original / commissioned research)
- giving expert written or oral evidence to government consultations / parliamentary committees / individual policymakers or regulators
- employing current / former politicians / decision makers
- hospitality / entertaining of policymakers / politicians
- briefing decision makers (face-to-face or in writing)
- advertising to mobilise public support
- direct mail to supporters (and encouraging them to use direct mail to contact policymakers).

Whilst this is an impressive list as the examples in this book will show, it is far from a full list. It focuses, as you would expect from a communications consultant, on the key communications activities, but there are other important aspects, not least having streams of funding.

The reality is that campaigners use a wider range of tools including legal avenues. They look to target the weak spots in their opponents, demonstrating their failures especially when this comes up against any public statements.

There can be a 'say-do' gap between what, for instance, a company says it does and what it delivers in reality. That can be down to a mistake, misfortune or, in some cases, misinformation. But whether by accident or design, it needs to be called out and that is where campaigners fulfil an often much-needed role.

They are not the only ones that can call it out. Journalists and politicians can also do this, but campaigners often keep on the case for longer and that constant holding of an organisation to account can make all the difference.

Companies are aware of the danger of that potential gap between communications and performance. They may have a laudable aim but take their time to achieve it. That is acceptable if sufficient progress is being made, in a timely manner, and audiences are kept informed.

A failure to keep audiences up to date creates potential friction and increases risk especially if there is already an active campaign maintaining a spotlight.

In many cases, businesses consider risks but attribute potential damage to regulatory action or, in some cases, political action. They do not, however, consider how an activist campaign could be given ammunition and momentum. If a campaign already exists, then it becomes part of the discussion, but few businesses think that they could be the target of a campaign unless they operate in a 'traditional' target area such as extractive industries.

Targeting government

It is not just businesses that are the focus of activist activity. Governments are often targeted because of their failure to take action. They also have the power to change the activity of others by changing laws, regulations, taxation etc. Governments can shift behaviours and actions both through soft power and hard actions.

In the UK, a very effective campaign targeting the government was led by Manchester United and England footballer, Marcus Rashford. He certainly grabbed much of the media attention because of his existing profile but the work was very far from being that of one person.

Rashford had been an ambassador of FareShare since March 2020.[3] FareShare redistributes surplus food to charities that turn it into meals.

At the start of the Covid-19 outbreak, FareShare launched an appeal calling for donations, food and volunteers. Rashford heard about the appeal and especially its campaign seeking to help vulnerable children over the school summer holidays.

Rashford's involvement in the campaign was deeply personal, and this element was highlighted in the media. He used free school meals as a child.

Rashford made a number of financial donations to help children access food from FareShare and, through social media, suggested his followers to donate and support as well.

But there was also activity focusing on the government. In particular, he launched a Child Food Poverty Taskforce, a group of more than 15 organisations to support a National Food Strategy.

He focused his activity, and that of his followers, on government ministers calling them out for failing to support vulnerable children. The then Prime Minister, Boris Johnson, was forced to U-turn on existing policies by Rashford, supported by other charities, media, the opposition Labour Party but even some of his own Members of Parliament. Rashford made the government look so out of step with public opinion that they caved in.

There is no doubt that Rashford made child food poverty a household issue. It gained a prominence that it had not had before. He successfully used his profile and personal experience to exert influence.

There was plenty to learn from the campaign. There is no doubt that Rashford is a special footballing talent but his campaign to extend free school meals to those who receive them to include the school holidays has been a masterclass in campaigning. He pushed, cajoled and secured action from the government.

What lessons can we take?

- Using the tools at his disposal – for such a campaign, the weight of numbers can be important. A petition on the UK Parliament website received over 1 million signatures and led to a debate in Parliament.
- Effective social media use – so not just putting a statement out on Twitter but engaging directly with politicians and calling them out on their position. Conservative Steve Baker MP was challenged by Rashford to open up to comments so that they could engage in a debate.

- Hold the government to account – always try to play the government's own agenda and comments back at them to help exert pressure. Do the same with individual politicians as well.
- Make common cause with those who support your aims – Rashford has been happy to work with others to drive for success in the campaign and hasn't been precious about any 'ownership' issues. That is not just about other campaigners. The private sector is involved as well, for instance, with the Child Food Poverty Taskforce which was set up. Nestle, for one, were happy to talk publicly about their involvement and it is obvious to see the benefits for them.
- Don't waste time reinventing existing campaigns – the creation of the Taskforce allowed Rashford to get existing experience in and secure advice wherever it may be needed.
- Ensure the message hits home – the aims of the campaign have to seem achievable and resonate with people, which also helps to build support.
- Maintaining the pressure over time – it is difficult to keep large numbers of people motivated over a long period of time. He has managed it so far, but he needs to keep giving supporters useful things to do.
- Sometimes a blanket approach can be right – targeted is normally more effective but sometimes a blanket approach, for instance to all MPs, can be right. Don't always rule it out as ineffective.

All this is to say nothing of Rashford himself who embodied the campaign and has a very personal connection to it. His experience means that he did not detract from the campaign and wasn't simply a paid influencer of the type some campaigns will be attracted to. This was a personal crusade.

Rashford also had to keep his own brand in good shape as well. A Covid-19 failing or personal indiscretion would have consequences for the campaign as well.

Government reaction

It has to be remembered that political audiences and governments are less likely to engage with groups that pursue activities that are in a legally grey area, and certainly not if illegal, or activities that inflict high levels of disruption.

Even groups that conduct activities that are legal but inflict disruption can find themselves in the political wilderness. This may not be damaging in the longer term and some campaigns that seek to inflict disruption certainly gain media attention. That can help to raise the profile of an issue and mean that public awareness is heightened. But there is a tipping point.

Take the example of trade unions in the UK. In the face of strikes by a number of largely public sector professions in the UK in 2022 and 2023, the Conservative Government proposed a series of reforms.

Much of this comes down to a simple equation as far as governments are concerned. Are the public more likely to support striking public sector workers or would they prefer the strong hand of government to take charge? In the Conservative Party's 2019 General Election manifesto it stated:

> We will require that a minimum service operates during transport strikes. Rail workers deserve a fair deal, but it is not fair to let the trade unions undermine the livelihoods of others.[4]

In the face of more strikes this has now gone further. Then Business Secretary, Rt Hon Grant Shapps MP said:

> As well as protecting the freedom to strike, the government must also protect life and livelihoods. While we hope that voluntary agreements can continue to be made in most cases, introducing minimum safety levels – the minimum levels of service we expect to be provided – will restore the balance between those seeking to strike and protecting the public from disproportionate disruption.[5]

So minimum service levels, which are already insisted upon in some countries, are being considered for a range of public sector services, not just transport.

Whilst this type of action, or rhetoric, may work well with some audiences, it does little to stem the tide of industrial action in the short term.

It does though illustrate the type of reaction that can result from high-profile, disruptive pressure being applied on the general public. Governments can react if they believe that they, not the campaigners, have public support.

Governments will also take regulatory action if they feel an organisation or sector is not moving fast enough or reacting to government encouragement. Social media companies are a case in point. Poor behaviour is highlighted by campaigns, government encourages change, campaigns show that the change is not happening or is too slow, governments take greater regulatory, or other, action. Effective activists know and understand how to lobby governments.

Information

One of the key challenges for all those involved is finding out what is really going on – getting information.

I spoke to Robert Blood, founder and managing director of SIGWATCH. SIGWATCH is the world's leading consultancy on global activism. It tracks NGO campaigning to predict emerging issues and help companies and governments understand the trends that are shaping their markets.

We began by looking at the sort of information companies need to consider when engaging with activists and how they best prepare themselves. Robert suggested that they:

1   Conduct a thorough assessment: Companies should conduct a thorough assessment of the activists' concerns and the potential impact on their business operations. This can help them develop a comprehensive strategy to address the concerns and minimize risks. For example, companies operating in industries with a history of environmental controversies, like oil and gas, should conduct a non-technical risk assessment of their operations and develop an action plan to address environmental and social concerns.

2   Build relationships (or at least connections): Companies should build relationships with activist groups and engage in ongoing dialogue to better understand their concerns and perspectives. This can help companies to address concerns proactively and avoid negative publicity and foreground emerging issues. For example, Walmart has established a sustainability consortium that includes environmental activists to help it address environmental concerns in its operations.

3   Communicate effectively: Companies should develop effective communication strategies that clearly communicate their position and actions to address concerns. This can help to build trust and credibility with activists and the public. Starbucks claims to have established an open-door policy for animal welfare activists to engage in dialogue about its sourcing policies and practices (this has not stopped some groups continuing to be highly critical of the company on issues such as sow gestation crates and charging more for non-dairy milk).

4   Demonstrate a commitment to change: Companies should demonstrate their commitment to change by taking concrete actions to address concerns raised by activists. This can help to build a positive relationship with activists and the public. This underpins the significance of Unilever's leadership on sustainability. The company has not only reduced its environmental footprint, it has set out a long term plan with explicit targets to address a wide range of issues raised by NGOs.

5   Understand the issues, listen actively: Companies should have a good understanding of the issues that activists are advocating for. This means not only conducting research and gathering information to inform their responses but establishing a dialogue with a wide range of experts, from activist groups to academics, to better understand the concerns and arguments.

6   Be transparent: Companies should be transparent in their communications with activists, and be willing to share information about their operations, policies, and decision-making processes. The publication of annual sustainability reports is the bare minimum here. Sharing data and plans with stakeholders and experts is really important for building trust that the organisation is serious.

7   Respond appropriately: Companies should be prepared to respond to the concerns of activists in a timely and appropriate manner. This may

involve making changes to their practices, policies or operations. Keeping a weather eye out for developments such as new campaigns or emerging issues is vital to avoid being caught off-guard, and to be able to plan for change in a responsible way.

8   Respectful engagement: Companies should engage with activists in a respectful and constructive manner, without resorting to hostile or confrontational tactics. Sometimes this is hard when groups are deliberately confrontational, but often this is only happening because activists are frustrated at the lack of meaningful response. Also remember that for every activist abseiling down your building, there are likely thousands of people who support what they are doing and will be influenced by how you respond.

9   Consider the impact on stakeholders: Companies should always consider the potential impact of their engagement with activists on other stakeholders, such as customers and investors, and especially employees. Staff generally want to feel they belong to an organisation with integrity, and this includes behaviours and attitudes to the issues raised by ESG considerations. Younger employees may be particularly affected by negative allegations. At the height of the boycott of Nestle in the 1980s, called to protest the marketing of infant formula in developing countries, the most significant impact was reportedly not on the firm's sales, but on its ability to recruit high-quality graduates out of university.

But, I asked, what do companies typically get wrong during their engagement with activists?

When engaging with activists, companies can sometimes make mistakes that can undermine the effectiveness of their response or even exacerbate the situation. Here are some common mistakes that firms make when engaging with activists:

1   Ignoring or dismissing activist groups: Companies may choose to ignore activist groups or dismiss their concerns, which can further escalate the situation. For example, Nike was criticised for initially ignoring concerns raised by human rights activists over the use of sweatshop labour in its supply chain in the early 90s until negative media articles began appearing (including the now famous 1996 piece in *Time* magazine which included a photo of a 12-year-old Pakistani boy sewing a Nike football). By 2002 the firm had started auditing its suppliers.

2   Engaging in defensive tactics: Companies may adopt defensive tactics like legal action or public relations campaigns that can backfire and damage their reputation. In the US, the oil company Chevron was criticised for mounting an aggressive legal campaign against

Indigenous activists and their American lawyer who were seeking billions of dollars of damages over pollution in Ecuador. Later Chevron ran extensive advertising campaigns arguing that it was respecting communities where it operated.

3 Failing to listen and address concerns: Companies may fail to listen to the concerns of activist groups and take corrective actions. For example, over the last two decades several commonly used chemicals, from certain food additives to Teflon-coated wraps, have been abandoned by major firms in response to raising public disquiet, yet activists were raising concerns with these firms before public awareness started to rise. Earlier action could have saved unnecessary damage to brand values.

4 Taking a confrontational approach: Companies may take a hardline stance against activist groups, which can escalate the situation and create negative publicity. In 2010 Nestle was singled out by Greenpeace over Indonesian palm oil in a highly emotive video linking its iconic KitKat chocolate bar to the murder of orangutans. Instead of engaging seriously with the environmental group, Nestle sued YouTube to take down Greenpeace's video. This move, far from quenching the reputational fire, just added fuel by turning it into an argument about suppression of free speech. Greenpeace's video was uploaded on multiple alternative platforms and Nestle's discomfort became the topic of media articles across the world.

5 Failing to communicate effectively: Companies may fail to communicate their efforts and progress in addressing concerns raised by activist groups, which can create a perception of apathy and inaction. For example, Coca-Cola arguably failed to effectively communicate its efforts to address concerns raised by activist groups about water usage from its bottling operations, so that it became accused of single-handedly causing Indian farmers to run out of water.

6 Failing to follow through: Companies making promises to activists but failing to follow through on their commitments erodes trust and credibility. It is for this reason that campaigners now only take corporate pledges seriously if accompanied by time-defined quantitative targets.

7 Treating activists as a monolithic group: Companies that assume that all activists share the same views or goals can overlook important nuances or miss opportunities for engagement. This is true even on the same issue. For example, at face value, conservation and organic farming campaigners are both hostile to pesticides. Dig deeper, and it becomes apparent that while the organic farming activists reject pesticides on principle, most conservation groups are far more concerned about the effect of pesticides on biodiversity and wildlife. This difference provides an opportunity for the

pesticide makers to engage meaningfully with at least some of their critics by agreeing how to reduce the impact of their products.

8   Failing to listen: Companies that do not listen to the concerns and demands of activists can miss important insights and opportunities for improvement. In almost all the topics on which they campaign, activists not only lead public opinion, they establish principles which sooner or later become mainstream. We have seen this in our own lifetimes on issues such as gender and LGBTQIA+ rights, racial justice, air pollution, plastics, climate change and animal welfare (i.e. testing cosmetics on animals, once commonplace, is now largely outlawed or abandoned). Listening to activists not only helps firms avoid unnecessary reputational damage, it gives them a glimpse into the future, for which they can prepare.

Robert and I discussed the rise of ESG (environmental, social and governance) and whether businesses really understand what is involved?

ESG is an approach to investing that takes into account the environmental, social, and governance performance of companies. The rise of ESG reflects a growing awareness among investors and businesses of the importance of these issues, and the need to take them into account when making investment and business decisions.

Overall, the rise of ESG has to be seen as a positive development, as it can help to drive progress on important environmental and social issues and promote more sustainable and responsible business practices. However, the effectiveness of ESG will depend on whether businesses truly understand what is involved and are committed to making meaningful changes.

Some businesses may see ESG as a box-ticking exercise or a way to improve their reputation, rather than as a fundamental shift in their approach to sustainability and responsible business. This can lead to superficial or incomplete ESG strategies that do not have a meaningful impact on the environment or society.

To be effective, businesses need to take a holistic and strategic approach to ESG and integrate it into their overall business strategy and operations. This can involve setting ambitious sustainability goals, engaging with stakeholders, developing a clear and comprehensive ESG strategy, and measuring and reporting on progress.

Overall, the rise of ESG represents an important shift in the way that businesses and investors approach sustainability and responsible business. However, its success will depend on whether businesses truly understand what is involved and are committed to making meaningful changes.

We ended our conversation by asking why companies can often be seen as being 'behind' activists and how they can best lead rather than simply being reactive.

Activists will always be 'ahead' of companies on ESG issues, but this does not prevent companies leading their sector, for example, Walmart, Nestle, H&M, and Unilever. This is how they did it:

1   Set ambitious goals: Companies should set ambitious goals to reduce their environmental and social impacts, such as reducing greenhouse gas emissions, water use, and waste. These goals should be based on science and aligned with global targets, such as the UN Sustainable Development Goals.
2   Develop a clear strategy: Companies should develop a clear and comprehensive sustainability strategy that outlines their approach to addressing environmental and social issues. This strategy should be integrated into the company's overall business strategy and operations.
3   Engage stakeholders: Companies should engage with stakeholders, such as customers, employees, investors, and NGOs, to understand their expectations and priorities around sustainability. This can help to inform the company's sustainability strategy and goals.
4   Innovate and collaborate: Companies should innovate and collaborate with others to develop new solutions to environmental and social challenges. This can involve partnerships with suppliers, customers, NGOs, and governments to drive progress at scale.
5   Report on progress: Companies should report regularly on their sustainability performance, including progress against goals and any challenges or setbacks. This can help to build transparency and accountability and demonstrate the company's commitment to making a positive impact.
6   Support policy and regulation: Companies should support policy and regulation that advances sustainability, such as carbon pricing or renewable energy mandates. This can help to create a level playing field and drive systemic change.

Challenging the very term 'stakeholders', Andrea Hagelgans of Edelman said that it is too broad a term as it fails to capture differences; internal stakeholders are not homogenous but diverse.[6] Problems arise when organisations do not fully understand the audiences relevant to them. Without information, concerns cannot be addressed and problems not seen off before they arise. Activist attacks can be avoided with better information, as Robert highlighted.

That also involves knowing what is going on around you as well. The sorts of challenges faced by others in your sector and how they are responding and reacting. What sorts of pressures are being applied on them? They could well come your way as well.

'Insider' vs 'outsider'

Many campaigns are considered to be one organisation, or group of supporters, against a defined target that could be a single organisation or an entire sector. An outsider campaign. But campaigns are just as likely to be fought within organisations making it an 'insider' campaign.

Some of the most effective work in recent years has been undertaken by often initially small groups seeking to force change within the organisation they work for.

In many countries, trade unions have fought these campaigns for a long time but for some companies, often in the tech sector, they have sought to avoid allowing trade unions to be established, especially in the US.

This has led to internal campaigns flourishing. That also instinctively makes sense. The views from inside an organisation appear to resonate more with external audiences. Criticisms hit home harder, and support defends well. Employees can be an organisation's most valuable advocates but also the critics that can do the most damage.

If an organisation cannot be trusted to look after their own employees, then the question can be asked, how can they be trusted with any other element of their operations? These insider voices also have access to information sometimes denied to those outside. That makes them uniquely placed to expose poor behaviour on the basis of evidence.

The rise of internal battles has been some of the most damaging for companies in the tech sector. There have been campaigns in Microsoft, Google, Uber and a whole range of other companies. Janneke Parrish describes the Apple Together campaign in Chapter 3.

Speaking to the Masters of Scale podcast, Microsoft's Satya Nadella suggested that 'Your definition of success should include the community around you'.[7]

A further clarification could be that success is also about the community within you. Reid Hoffman, in the same podcast, made a similar point when saying that all employees have a role in delivering that business's success and so are 'acting in a way that serves the mission'.

But that implies that all employees also have a role in holding that company to account for its behaviour as well which is something we have seen in relation to many businesses. The fight to hold companies to account can come from within as much as it can from outside.

The pressure of the sector

There is no standing alone for any organisation or business. Whilst it may be possible to highlight the good work that they undertake and deliver, there also needs to be an appreciation that the wider sector in which they operate also has an impact.

Certainly, as far as governments are concerned, problems caused by a few players in a market can lead to action against all. That is part of what also makes activists, lobbyists.

That blanket approach by government may not seem entirely fair for many businesses but the only way to overcome that is through their own direct engagement. The blunt instrument of new legislation can at least be tempered by explaining to government what the reality is for the vast majority of a sector.

That only works, however, if that really is the case. An organisation may choose to adopt a market leading position on, for instance, protecting the environment. But if others in the sector are failing to keep pace or, worse still, engaging in practices that are detrimental then government will take action that impacts everyone.

Being ahead of the competition could offer some protection. The government action could be to impose standards that the business adhered to long ago. That cannot be guaranteed however. Governments may choose instead to take a gold standard approach to demonstrate to voters how they are holding a sector to account.

Whatever the situation, government has to know what best practice looks like, what is possible and what can be achieved. That calls for strong individual voices as well as a collective voice.

These are arguments for leading and being proactive for an organisation but also, where possible, looking to encourage those around them as well.

There will be activist campaigns that look to show-up failings. One such campaign in the UK has been led by Feargal Sharkey OBE, Vice Chair of River Action but better known to many as the former lead singer of Irish band The Undertones. Sharkey has been fighting against the discharge of sewage into Britain's inland and coastal waters. His efforts, along with other campaigners, have frightened Britain's water companies and have led the government to issue a number of strategies to try to deal with the problem. There is no doubt that Sharkey's profile has helped maintain an interest in the issue, but so has the use of data to show that the problem is continuing, as well as real-life examples. Maintaining momentum can be difficult but Sharkey and his fellow campaigners have achieved that.[8]

An activist age?

The changing nature of information availability, it could be suggested, has shifted the relationship between people and organisations. Transparency has increased and with it comes the availability of information through official sources. But as more information is released, the demands for more increase as well.

There is no doubt that the rise of social media has contributed to these demands. There is both more direct access on the part of individuals but also an enhanced capability to act collectively.

The reality for many is that they do not mind being involved but like to be directed and organised. There remains a role for organisations to bring like-minded people together, to provide information and to suggest ideas for action.

Political parties may not have the membership numbers of the past but other civil society organisations have never been more popular.

The rise of the hyper local groups has been facilitated by online activity. Who is not now a member of a WhatsApp group for their local street? The more bound in one is, the greater the sense of local community that can be developed.

If political parties want to facilitate feelings of community engagement or businesses want to be part of their communities then they could do worse than being openly, and transparently, involved in such groups or, at least, get information to them. Political campaigning has certainly picked up on this. There is a trust amongst friends that is often lacking when it comes to politicians and the media. Businesses tend to fair a little better but as the Edelman Trust Barometer has shown over the years that can vary as well.

If we take into account the profile of some activist campaigns, such as the environmental movement, and the apparent growth in youth activism then it could be considered that we live in an 'activist age'. It is a reality that governments, businesses and communities have to live with.

Global events such as Covid may even have brought greater activist unity between age groups.[9] Greta Thunberg is arguably the poster person for activism and has become a lightning rod for criticism and all the scrutiny that comes with that. There is no doubt that has generated additional profile. Who would not be interested in a public spat where a teenage activist schools a US President?

Gen Z, those born between 1997 and 2012, appear ready to take up activism and fight for their beliefs.[10] The fact they are happy to employ technology in their activism should be no surprise as they are considered to be the first generation to grow up with access to the internet and technology. They are used to having power literally in their hands.

Gen Z are considered to be more active than previous generations, but the reality is that previous generations too have taken up causes and been active. The difference with this generation appears to be the consistency of activism. They are comfortable advocating for numerous social and political issues such as climate change, LGBTQIA+ rights and racial equality. This focus on 'marginalised communities' appears engrained and puts them on a direct collision course with those who wish to question such rights. According to the World Economic Forum, Gen Z's focus on sustainability is rubbing off on others.[11]

As with younger generations, there is an undoubted thirst for speed in change. Maybe every generation that comes forward are just that little more challenging of the ones that have come before, meaning that Gen Alpha will be even more challenging.

According to some studies, Gen Z do appear to have priorities based around purpose, and social responsibility which impacts on those they buy from and do business with. Companies are, therefore, having to take notice and this has an impact on their behaviour and approach.

In this type of Activist Age, working together to achieve an aim is perfectly acceptable. It is difficult to argue whether civil society is healthier now than in the past because there are so many variable factors. But with apparently more opportunities for engagement, an increased ability to engage and collaborate through online tools and some very vocal and high-profile advocates, many will feel that civil society is stronger.

There is, of course, no guaranteeing that rights only increase. It has been suggested that rights have been removed in the UK.

The types of tactics employed by the likes of Extinction Rebellion are 'a real product of the government's action to restrict protest in recent years' claimed Jodie Beck, Head of Policy and Campaigns at Liberty. Speaking on the *New Statesman* podcast,[12] she suggested that the introduction of new police powers, extending criminality and restricting assemblies, has contributed to the shift to 'more urgent methods of protest'.

The UK Government introduced the Police, Crime, Sentencing and Courts Act in 2022 so that, along with previous laws, the police can:

> impose any type of condition on a public procession or public assembly necessary to prevent: significant impact on persons or serious disruption to the activities of an organisation by noise; serious disorder; serious damage to property; serious disruption to the life of the community; or if the purpose of the persons organising the protest is the intimidation of others with a view to compelling them not to do an act they have a right to do, or to do an act they have a right not to do.[13]

However, the Government then admitted that:

> Recent changes in the tactics employed by certain protesters, for example gluing themselves to buildings or vehicles, blocking roads, tunnelling under land that is subject to development, and obstructing access to buildings such as oil refineries and newspaper printing works, have highlighted some gaps in current legislation.[14]

As a result, it introduced a new Public Order Act. In other words, as the government changed the law, activists changed tactics; as a result, the government felt compelled to introduce more laws and further restrict activity.

Such government action focuses simply on the outcomes of activism and whether they are perceived as disruptive to the general public or not. It ignores the nature of those who are undertaking the activism who could be students or retired people. One of the perceived characteristics of the environmental movement is how older people are getting involved as well. It is not just the preserve of Gen Z.

The Civil Liberties Union for Europe (Liberties), point out that it 'is a misconception that in order to be an activist, you need to be an expert on a topic or working in a professional capacity. Anyone who cares about a cause and participates in collective action to bring about change is considered an activist. Within a collective movement, there are many different roles that activists can take on to be effective in achieving their mission'.

They suggest that these are:

- citizens
- reformers: who will work within existing institutions
- rebels: prepared to work outside of such institutions and demand change of them
- change agents: who focus on educating the public.[15]

Whilst the young may be the largest group of activists, it is no longer solely their preserve. Student demonstrations may remain popular but people of all ages, ethnicities and backgrounds are increasingly involved in activism.

As the Black Lives Matter movement proves, the fight against systemic racism and inequality attracts a range of diverse voices, not just the 'usual suspects'.

This, in turn, changes activism's political profile. If activism is no longer the preserve of small groups but is 'mainstream' then the way in which governments need to listen changes. If the groups were small, then they could be ignored. This is now less and less the case. If ordinary voters are involved, in potentially significant numbers, then politicians need to take notice.

The UK government's legislative actions fail to reflect a widening of the activist base and coming together of ages.

Young people are still more motivated to take part in action on climate change.[16] In many ways that is completely understandable as they are the ones who will have to live with the consequences if action is not taken.

However, if we look at Extinction Rebellion in the UK then we start to see a different picture starting to emerge. Research[17] shows that:

- Activists who took part in Extinction Rebellion's major protests were overwhelmingly middle class, highly educated and southern.
- Extinction Rebellion activists found to have a more diverse age profile than other environmental protests.
- 85 per cent of those who took part in the action in London in 2019 were educated to degree level.[18]

Although the estimates of the numbers involved vary, there is no doubt that marches against Brexit and against the war in Iraq brought out very large numbers of people.

The media love a story about the types of people arrested during activist action. If they were 'just' young people or students, then there would not be much of a story. But in recent arrests at Insulate Britain, Just Stop Oil and Extinction Rebellion protests, the stories of grandmothers being arrested made them interesting. It would be foolish to extrapolate too much from any of these individual stories but there seems to be a general theme of generations campaigning together especially when it comes to protecting the climate.

Some issues have the ability to capture the wider imagination often after some initial campaigning to bring it to the attention of the public. The support for Marcus Rashford's campaign for free school meals is one example, as mentioned above, but so was the campaign against the proposed privatisation of the Forestry Commission which would have 'sold off' the country's forests. It appeared that the then Conservative and Liberal Democrat coalition UK government failed to appreciate the feeling generated and expressed in protests, and across the media. It led one government minister to say 'we got this one wrong' as they reversed position.

This is important for businesses, governments and the activists themselves. There is the chance of groups working more closely together and campaigns that cannot be neatly pigeon-holed.

Activist campaigns are not solely the preserve of, often non-voting, students. Activism is instead a more attractive option for many.

Businesses need to think more broadly about political activists and, therefore, the types of action they could face. They should not fall into lazy and outdated stereotypes or preconceptions.

But it is not a universal story of increasing activism. Volunteering in the UK is generally stable but has seen a significant dip in recent years according to NCVO figures.[19] It is a similar story in the US.[20]

There are a number of reasons why this may be the case but one could be that the competition for activism is much higher. There are more opportunities for people to be active and they can be focused on the issues that motivate them most. Simply, there is competition for activists.

But we can also see that charitable giving is up in the US[21] and UK.[22] It could be that some have offset their volunteering through financial contributions. It is a very complicated picture.

I discussed the changing nature of activism with Dr Lynn Bennie who leads courses at the University of Aberdeen including 'Protest to Power: How to Campaign and Win' and an MSc in 'Political Activism and Campaigning'.[23]

We started by considering how activism changed and developed.

There has been an increase in activism and movement-type behaviour. This is sparked by societal problems (inequality in various forms, climate change), as has always been the case, but now this is combined with modern forms of communication. New technology has become a useful organising tool for campaigners, and it helps create movement networks. There's a cyclical nature to protest activism – it occurs when times are tough and can come round again in different forms – think civil rights and BLM, feminism of 1960s/70s and MeToo. For some campaigns, such as those focused on climate change, there's a sense of urgency that has intensified.

An issue that I highlight on the course is that you tend to have more activism at times of economic difficulty and distress. The genuine problems in society are more clearly displayed and that's what sparks that activity.

That, in turn, gives activism a sort of cyclical nature. At the moment we are living through economic troubles, so we see an uptick in activism. But there is also resource bias inherent in activism, which means that it's the people with skills, with money and with a good education tend to be the campaigners. The people who are actually campaigning are not necessarily people who are suffering from the problem. That means there is a middle-class bias and participation across the board, for those involved in campaign activity.

One theme of our course is that campaign activism (indeed, any form of political participation) tends to be dominated by people with resources, i.e., the economically well-resourced and well-educated. And young people tend to be *under*-represented. If we include digital activism in our analysis, then younger people are obviously more involved in this way. The recent climate activism has also appealed to younger people (Greta's army), but academic research shows that even here there is a typical 'profile' – middle-aged, well-educated, middle class (see report by Saunders et al. 2020).[24]

We considered whether climate change could be a more existential threat that breaks out of the economic cycle of activism so that if economic growth returns the level of activism would remain high.

I think climate change is something separate and standalone. The issues are existential and the challenges so severe with so many implications for the planet and people that it could maintain activism and also draw in some of the people who might not typically be involved. That could be true not least for young people.

We have seen a similar cycle in green movements and peace campaigners in the past. But climate change is now so severe and such a powerful sort of raw issue, I think, for many young people especially.

The reality is that although the impact of some protests can appear large and generate media interest, the numbers involved in campaigning is low.

We get all these images of the climate strikers, and the activity is widely reported. But whilst it looks like a lot of activity it was still a very small minority of young people who were participating. So, I think we always need to.

Especially in a period of economic growth, I suggested that this could enhance the prospect of more radical or more aggressive activist action to maintain the pressure. Lynn agreed with this, pointing to the need for groups to reinvent their tactics to maintain attention.

But I would say that that's probably not new. The story of Greenpeace shows how tactics need to change. It became ever more radical but that eventually backfired, and audiences lost faith in them, particularly around the Brent Spar incident.[25]

So effective activism needs to focus on innovation in tactics?

Yes, they need to constantly try to think of ways that they will get attention for the cause. They cannot keep just doing the same thing. That makes activism a very creative industry. To maintain attention that can mean coming up with different ways to shock, sometimes disrupt.

Greenpeace became more of an 'insider' type group and has worked with companies. Some protestors prefer to remain 'outside'. Lynn believes that the distinction between 'insider' and 'outsider' groups is a really important one because groups are aware of their status and they 'craft their tactics accordingly'. Some, particularly younger, activists believe that lobbying a politician is straightforward, Lynn suggested. The reality is that politicians do not necessarily listen, especially if the activists only represent a small group and / or want radical change. The activists need to understand the setting and the politics.

Securing that sort of influence over decision-making is about engaging with a range of stakeholders. Not just politicians but also businesses, a realisation that shareholder activists had many years ago. A shift in the behaviour of large companies can then have an impact on others. There can be a ripple effect to other organisations that start to move because they need to do business with one that insists on behaviours of a certain type or that believe that reputationally they could miss out because another organisation has effectively stolen a march on them.

For Lynn this means that 'there are different spheres that campaigners may be focused on', and that this requires resources, but also understanding about who the decision-makers really are, where the power really lies.

This can sometimes be really difficult to pin down. Pointing to the work of Professor James Tilley on social movements,[26] Lynn explained how the success of an activist campaign or protest movement can be challenging to prove. 'It's never something that we, as political scientists, are ever going to be able to really measure'. Tilley points to the possibility of indirect change.

But, for Lynn, even if change does not come about then those who take part can feel collective involvement, an enhanced sense of agency through taking action. That does not mean that the change comes about but it can be important to people that they can protest.

There can also be moral dilemmas involved in designing actions. Higher profiler campaigns, such as those conducted by Just Stop Oil, involve negative consequences for some. These have the potential to turn people against the campaign. But the same can be said of more established forms of campaigning such as those conducted by trade unions. Strikes can hit all aspects of life – health, education, transport etc. But that very disruption ensures that the issues have a chance to be aired to a wider audience across the media.

> I would always defend people's right to be passionate, protest and agitate because it is a fundamental democratic right.

When it comes to the success of a campaign, Lynn explains:

> The meaning of success is not always clear, particularly in the case of social movements with diverse aims. However, campaigns that are successful tend to have the following ingredients: a clear aim, well-articulated; resources, perhaps from donations; knowledge of supporters; thought-through campaign techniques / tactics; knowledge of the decision-makers and access points in the political system; and effective leadership. Leadership is widely debated in some groups, as movement politics tends to emphasise grassroots, bottom-up type activity. However, even groups like Extinction Rebellion have and require leaders. In the end, if campaigners get media attention, gain widespread support and persuade decision-makers they have a strong case, this can be viewed as success.
>
> A good example is the Assisted Dying Campaign in Scotland. This campaign has been successful, and has been run by two or three people, who are very good at what they do, and they're good at talking to politicians. They are good at mobilising, at communicating and at persuading politicians to take this difficult issue on.

Effective leadership is a theme that Lynn returns to as research shows that groups require organisation and people in the right place with good communication skills and an ability to work with others. Ally Thomson, Director of Dignity in Dying Scotland, is one such individual that Lynn points to as she has 'all the skills necessary to persuade and not to scare someone off from what is a very delicate issue'. 'The individuals, the skills and knowledge, the expertise of those involved in the campaign, they really matter'.

Sometimes having a figurehead who does not fit the usual mould, such as Greta Thunberg, can capture the imagination and motivate people.

> I would say that campaign repertoires have become more varied. Social media, for example, didn't exist in the early days of Greenpeace campaigns or the women's rights movement. Campaign events and tactics have become increasingly colourful and creative – think Just Stop Oil[27] – but all these forms of protest are designed to attract attention and to mobilise support, in the hope that change in decision-making might occur. This is a tried and tested formula for political activists. Now, though, there's the added ingredient of social media – where images of a traditional style protest can go viral. But campaigns involve a vast range of tactics – from public protest to behind the scenes lobbying and 'conversations'. Groups make a judgement about the opportunities available to them and design their campaigns accordingly. For example, a campaign to stop closure of local libraries in Aberdeen has involved a social media campaign, encouraging people to contact local councillors, and traditional protest like organised rallies and public meetings.

On the future of activism:

> That's a difficult question! We should acknowledge that the vast majority of people in advanced democracies will never take part in campaign activism, at least not beyond liking a post on social media. However, I think that younger generations now view campaign activism as a kind of 'norm'. There is no doubt that the world faces many real challenges and younger people are knowledgeable about these problems, partly due to information spread through new technology. And there's a perception that young people need to sort out problems created (or at least not solved) by previous generations. This has the potential for even more radical activism.

Tactics will also change as technology continues to evolve and that will, in all likelihood, mean that huge funds are not required. Instead, with sufficient numbers of people involved, they can concentrate more on trying to broaden their scope in terms of actions, the range of potential supporters and the activist base away from just being the 'usual suspects'. That could bring a campaign more into everyday consciousness of more people.

Lynn believes that there needs to be greater focus on what a group or campaign actually achieves. If this is unclear, then 'there is a risk that you have a downward spiral of demobilisation. So rather than continued recruitment and continued pressure, it goes away, because people lose faith in the ability of it to actually make a change. That is another reason why leaders are important. They can communicate the successes, and the impact being achieved, recognising the effort and time commitment involved in being an effective activist.

With large campaigns it can be difficult to draw a connection between it and the actual delivery of change. To help counteract that, many campaigns now produce self-help campaigning guides. This breaks down the activity to make it more manageable and achievable.

That, in turn, means small steps towards a larger overarching aim can be taken and the benefits of activity clearly shown. It paints a picture to potential supporters about what can be achieved. 'They need to make clear the link between the aims of the campaign and what actually can be achieved. Many campaigns are very poor at that'.

Reflections

All sides involved are, in effect, considering communications. So that recognition in itself will mean that each can start to understand the other and how to respond effectively as well.

Businesses have decisions to make:

- Ignore the campaign.
- Defend themselves against the charges.
- Recognise that this is an issue, address it and make a virtue of it.

Activists, on the other hand, can:

- Maintain / increase the pressure, potentially using other tactics.
- Move to a new target if they think they have succeeded.
- Return to check on progress.

One of the most interesting and challenging books in the field of activism comes from Jon Alexander. In *Citizens: Why the Key to Fixing Everything Is All of Us* he suggests that we need to take the power of the citizen seriously. It is something that we can all play a role in because we are all citizens. If we do, then that changes the nature of businesses and governments. In the book, he suggests the tools needed to reinvent organisations, business and politics, helping us to transition to a citizen society: 'In the early 21st Century, the Consumer Story is collapsing under the weight of its own contradictions, and the Citizen Story is emerging'.[28]

He posits that 'we are citizens by nature'[29] but that citizen-focused organisations need to be open, transparent, 'show their working' and invite participation.[30] This will enable them to regain trust. It is through our role as citizens that we will deliver the transformation needed to take us into the future.

Fundamentally, this needs engagement and contribution as well as action 'rather than a passive state of being or receiving'.[31]

Businesses and governments, and their agencies, can note this and change themselves or they can continue in a 'business as usual' approach. Any change has to reflect how best they can bring in citizens and thereby use their power.

He suggests that organisations need to employ three Ps:

- Purpose – what is the organisation trying to do in the world?
- Platform – what opportunities does the organisation create for participation?
- Prototype – consider the starting point rather than trying to transform an organisation in one go.[32]

Alexander suggests that many businesses now understand the role that purpose plays, but fewer have taken the next step to open themselves up to allow participation.

There are, according to Alexander, seven ways in which a business can encourage 'everyday participation':

- Tell stories – customer testimonials.
- Gather data – citizens as researchers.
- Share connections – share details about purpose.
- Contribute ideas – their experience and ideas.
- Give time – working with an organisation.
- Learn skills – which helps deliver a deeper relationship.
- Crowdfund – buying into a company.[33]

It should be repeated that governments need to consider such engagement and participation as well.

The challenge is huge but so too are the potential benefits.

But discussing this with me, Jon challenged the idea that there has been much change in the relationship between activists and businesses.

> I basically don't think the relationship between activists and businesses has really changed all that much, for all the hype and talk. Fundamentally, I think activists and businesses fear each other. Businesses see activists as a threat, and therefore as something to be managed and controlled; and activists are deeply suspicious of business and don't want to get too close. I don't think things have changed that much since the experience with Unilever I wrote about in my book, and I don't think they will while the dominant idea of the individual in society is the Consumer.

He went on to say that:

> As to best practice, one of the examples I'm most excited about is the work we've been involved with at the Body Shop, helping establish the

> Youth Collective within its governance structure. This idea of a company integrating activism into its governance, actively harnessing its capacity to create the space for the company to move into, is what I would like to see much more of.[34]

This work illustrates what can be achieved when activists and businesses think differently about their relationship.

> I think about citizens rather than activists, as I think the concept of activism is too adversarial, and itself tends to embed and sustain the fear dynamic. I write in the book about citizens creating and imagining, more than they reject and resist. The quote that I always think of is the Buckminster Fuller one; 'You never change things by fighting the existing reality. To change something, build a new model that makes the existing model obsolete'.
>
> A really good example of this is what we're doing with the People's Plan for Nature – but it's telling that we've really struggled to get businesses involved in this.[35]

For Jon:

> Businesses need to create and hold space for citizens to help them figure out how to fulfil their purpose in the future. The whole of part 3 of my book is about the 3 Ps of participatory organisations – this is the model I think businesses need to step into in order to become constructive participants in society (you could say corporate citizens) themselves.
>
> And I think asking how citizens can hold business to account is to ask completely the wrong question! Citizens should be involved in creating the parameters for business through participatory democracy processes. 'Holding to account' is a combative frame that I don't think helps.

Not only do businesses and activists need to think differently, but we all do.

A similarly challenging outlook, that suggests that the old ways of making decisions is coming to an end and that businesses and political institutions can no longer be relied upon, is offered by a shift to the 'Good Society'. This 'model' places an emphasis on the development of alliances across civil society and the state. Change comes from above and below with the state retaining a role in helping to 'join up, scale up, accelerate, replicate and project emerging forms of collaborate action to ensure they become the predominant form of "deciding and doing" in the 21st century'.[36]

Activists need to maintain a diverse range of campaigns if they are to overcome the challenges they face, as well as capturing the attention of both the intended audience and the general public.

The concept of an 'arms race' of activist activity, where campaigns strive to stay ahead of their audience and maintain interest, helps to maintain momentum but can end up with negative media coverage. But even that can still serve as a reminder that an issue needs to be addressed.

Yet maybe there is a tipping point after the initial shock tactic starts to fade from the memory and the general public focus more on the disruption to their lives. Consider the spate of disruptions at sporting events which gained attention but has now apparently faded in importance. Whether to continue with such actions can even bring dispute between groups. Extinction Rebellion may have made a commitment to the organisers of the London Marathon not to undertake action, but Just Stop Oil did not. Extinction Rebellion went even further and suggested that they would help to 'guard' the marathon as well.[37] Such approaches could well bring activists groups into conflict with one another and illustrates how they can be in competition with one another for attention, finance, or members / activists and how even groups with similar aims can diverge on approach.

For businesses and activists, there is no getting away from the importance of understanding their target audiences and tailoring their tactics accordingly. As with all good campaigns, they need to consider who their audiences are, what their timetables are, and how best to communicate with them. Neither businesses nor activists exist in a vacuum. The political context, especially, will significantly shape the chances of success.

Activists must appreciate the need to raise awareness, mobilise support and address the lack of unity within movements. But this provides valuable insight for businesses seeking to deal with an ever-evolving activist landscape and how they should respond.

Notes

1 Sam Glover and James Ozden, 'Literature review: Protest movement success factors', Social Change Lab, October 2022, p. 1, www.socialchangelab.org/_files/ugd/503ba4_e21c47302af942878411eab654fe7780.pdf

2 Pagefield, *Pagefield Perspectives: The Case for Campaigning*, November 2022, p. 12, www.pagefield.co.uk/wp-content/uploads/2022/11/Pagefield-Case-for-Campaigning.pdf

3 Read more about FareShare, Marcus Rashford and the campaign at https://fareshare.org.uk/marcus-rashford/

4 The Conservative and Unionist Party, 'Get Brexit done: Unleash Britain's potential', Manifesto 2019, p. 27, https://assets-global.website-files.com/5da42e2cae7ebd3f8bde353c/5dda924905da587992a064ba_Conservative%202019%20Manifesto.pdf

5 UK Government, 'Government invites unions to return to the table and call off strikes', press release, 5 January 2023, www.gov.uk/government/news/government-invites-unions-to-return-to-the-table-and-call-off-strikes

6 PRovoke Media podcast, 'Engaging your stakeholders on today's issues', 21 July 2022, www.provokemedia.com/latest/article/engaging-your-stakeholders-on-today's-social-issues

7 Masters of Scale podcast, 'Microsoft's Satya Nadella: Why we need re-founders', 13 September 2022, https://mastersofscale.com/satya-nadella-why-we-need-refounders/

8 For more details of Sharkey's campaigning work see Sean O'Neill, 'Feargal Sharkey: My campaign to clean up Britain's waterways', *The Times*, 21 December 2021, www.thetimes.com/uk/politics/article/feargal-sharkey-pollution-waterways-undertones-h3w5cxxcc

9 Amelia Hill, 'Age no barrier to activism: How UK's young and old built bonds in Covid', *The Guardian*, 17 November 2021, www.theguardian.com/world/2021/nov/17/age-no-barrier-to-activism-how-uks-young-and-old-built-bonds-in-covid

10 Megan Carnegie, 'Gen Z: How young people are changing activism', *BBC*, 8 August 2022, www.bbc.com/worklife/article/20220803-gen-z-how-young-people-are-changing-activism

11 Johnny Wood, 'Gen Z cares about sustainability more than anyone else – and is starting to make others feel the same', World Economic Forum, 18 March 2022, www.weforum.org/agenda/2022/03/generation-z-sustainability-lifestyle-buying-decisions/

12 New Statesman podcast, 'Can we stop the government criminalising protest? With Jodie Beck of Liberty', 6 February 2023, www.newstatesman.com/podcasts/new-statesman-podcast/2023/02/stop-government-criminalising-protest-jodie-beck-of-liberty-house-lords-strikes

13 Public Order Bill, Explanatory Notes, House of Commons, 11 May 2022, https://publications.parliament.uk/pa/bills/cbill/58-03/0008/en/220008en.pdf

14 Public Order Bill, Explanatory Notes, House of Commons, 11 May 2022, https://publications.parliament.uk/pa/bills/cbill/58-03/0008/en/220008en.pdf

15 Eleanor Brooks, 'What is activism: Definitions, types, role, examples, importance', *Liberties*, 15 August 2023, www.liberties.eu/en/stories/activism/44871

16 Alec Tyson, Brian Kennedy and Cary Funk, 'Gen Z, Millennials stand out for climate change activism, social media engagement with issue', Pew Research Center, 26 May 2021, www.pewresearch.org/science/2021/05/26/climate-engagement-and-activism/

17 C. Saunders, B. Doherty and G. Hayes, 'A new climate movement? Extinction Rebellion's activists in profile', CUSP Working Paper Series No. 25. 15 July 2020, https://cusp.ac.uk/themes/p/xr-study/

18 Aston University, 'Extinction Rebellion's activists more likely to be new to protesting, study shows', press release, 15 July 2020, www.aston.ac.uk/latest-news/extinction-rebellions-activists-more-likely-be-new-protesting-study-shows

19 NCVO, 'UK civil society almanac 2021', 1 September 2021, www.ncvo.org.uk/news-and-insights/news-index/uk-civil-society-almanac-2021/volunteering/#/

20 NP Source, 'Volunteering statistics and trends for nonprofits', https://nonprofitssource.com/online-giving-statistics/volunteering-statistics/

21 NP Source, 'The ultimate list of charitable giving statistics for 2023', https://nonprofitssource.com/online-giving-statistics/

22 NPT UK, 'Charitable giving statistics in the United Kingdom', www.nptuk.org/philanthropic-resources/uk-charitable-giving-statistics/

23 For clarity, I am also an Honorary Research Fellow in the Department of Politics and International Relations at the University of Aberdeen.

24 C. Saunders, B. Doherty and G. Hayes, 'A new climate movement? Extinction Rebellion's activists in profile', CUSP Working Paper Series No. 25. 15 July 2020, https://cusp.ac.uk/themes/p/xr-study/

25 For a useful overview see www.reutersevents.com/sustainability/business-strategy/brent-spar-battle-launched-modern-activism; and Steve John and Stuart Thomson, *New Activism and the Corporate Response*, Palgrave Macmillan, 2003

26 Professor James Tilley, 'What is the point of street protest', *BBC Radio 4*, 9 October 2022, www.bbc.co.uk/programmes/m001cpkk

27 A really informative discussion about Just Stop Oil and its approach can be heard at PR Week in an interview with Zoe Cohen, a spokesperson for the organisation, 'Beyond the noise: We're not trying to be popular – behind Just Stop Oil's comms strategy', 9 August 2023, www.prweek.com/article/1832766/ were-not-trying-popular--behind-just-stop-oils-comms-strategy-prweek-podcast

28 Jon Alexander. *Citizens: Why the Key to Fixing Everything Is All of Us*, Canbury Press, 2022, p. 19

29 Jon Alexander. *Citizens: Why the Key to Fixing Everything Is All of Us*, Canbury Press, 2022, p. 24

30 Jon Alexander. *Citizens: Why the Key to Fixing Everything Is All of Us*, Canbury Press, 2022, p. 25

31 Jon Alexander. *Citizens: Why the Key to Fixing Everything Is All of Us*, Canbury Press, 2022, p. 94

32 Jon Alexander. *Citizens: Why the Key to Fixing Everything Is All of Us*, Canbury Press, 2022, outlined on p. 159

33 Jon Alexander. *Citizens: Why the Key to Fixing Everything Is All of Us*, Canbury Press, 2022, pp. 197–204; and https://twitter.com/jonjalex/status/1532780342783909888

34 Georgina Caldwell, 'The Body Shop launches youth collective to amplify young voices', *Global Cosmetics News*, 20 September 2022, www.globalcosmeticsnews.com/the-body-shop-launches-youth-collective-to-amplify-young-voices/

35 For more details of the project see https://peoplesplanfornature.org/

36 Neal Lawson, '45° change: Transforming society from below and above', *Compass*, November 2018, www.compassonline.org.uk/publications/45o-change-transforming-society-from-below-and-above

37 Harry Poole, 'London Marathon 2023: Organisers receive "unique" assurances over planned protests', *BBC Sport*, 19 April 2023, www.bbc.co.uk/sport/athletics/65326353

Chapter 2

The power of communities

Local communities are external to an organisation but are often closely aligned with their interests. They can be a valuable supporter of an organisation or, if antagonised, one of their most powerful opponents. This can make them a highly motivated activist group.

These communities can be antagonised because of an externality imposed by the business. This could be everything from the adverse impact of existing operations (such as pollution), through to the development of a new project (supermarket, factory, infrastructure, etc.). This brings them together in common cause against the business.

Communities increasingly understand the power at their disposal through expert networks, and also learn from the experience and 'best practice' of other campaigns across the world.

Even if a local community lacks financial resources, they will use other options at their disposal, not least working with the media / social media to threaten reputations and exert as much pressure as possible.

During my time being involved in projects, it has become clear that local communities are more aware of the power that they have than ever before. This can sometimes be about the number of people involved but is often related to motivation, speed of movement and an improved understanding of how they can achieve their desired outcome. They often understand the political and planning processes as well as, if not better than, promoters.

The same levels of resources, not just financial, are not available to all communities. Each community have to consider how best they can achieve their aims and assess the resources that they have access to.

In some instances, their power builds over time as a campaign develops. In others, the impact of an organisation's operations or plans can instantly motivate people.

What is clear is that the idea that a developer or company can simply bring the weight of their own resources to bear to get their own way has long gone. Instead, there has been a recognition of the need to work together. But community groups are not afraid to call out failings when they happen.

DOI: 10.4324/9781003371908-3

What goes wrong?

Antagonism between a business and a local community can arise for a number of reasons, not least because the needs of the community are not considered or are insufficiently considered. That means when, for instance, a new project or development is suggested that the local community are not thought through in its design, that no account is taken of their potential requirements. Both of which lead to the imposition of solutions.

There is no doubt that there can be a touch of arrogance in some instances. A business will believe that they can simply impose their will or solution wherever they turn up. It takes an organised local community to stand up for themselves.

A study of local community views around major infrastructure conducted by consultancy Copper sought to capture the experience of local people living through the key phases of a project's lifecycle. The work found that the planning process for major projects is not well understood and that whilst construction is the most memorable phase, local communities feel that communication is poor.[1]

This led the report to suggest a series of recommendations:

- Involve people and communities early – identify concerns and develop community insight.
- Establish the project lifestyle – and communicate it.
- Communicate often – helps build relationships.
- Communicate clearly – avoid jargon and technical detail.
- Beware of construction – poor communication can spark reputational damage.[2]

In essence, the findings reinforce the idea that community action against the project can be avoided with good communication, good engagement, listening and a free flow of information. Where knowledge gaps appear, and where poor relationships develop, a project is less likely to succeed.

It is important that they are considered from the very outset of any project otherwise poor relationships become the order of the day, the project suffers and communities can miss out on their benefits.

Stansted Airport Watch

Airport expansion has been a controversial topic in the UK for many years. A combination of a lack of government clarity over policy and, more recently, environmental concerns have left many proposals to flounder.

It is, however, also where we can see the power of local community groups. Many communities have come together to try to block the expansion of airports in their area. That can be for proposed new runways, greater numbers of flights or around other forms of airport development, such as replacement terminals.

One such example, and one that shows how long campaigns can often go on for, is around the London Stansted proposals. The airport was acquired by Manchester Airport Group in 2013.

The airport sits just northeast of London and is a base for a large number of European low-cost carriers.

As the airport says:

> London Stansted is a growing business committed to sharing its success and making a lasting difference to our local communities. We're immensely proud of our commitment to Corporate Social Responsibility, which recognises the importance of responsible growth and our desire to be a trusted neighbour.
>
> As the major air transport hub in the region, we understand the importance of achieving our growth in a sustainable way. We also recognise that we need to deliver benefits locally, whilst being mindful of our effects on the community and environment.
>
> As we grow, we will continue advancing the positive opportunities afforded by the development of the airport, working in partnership with local people to support the things that really matter to them.[3]

But this has not stopped an active community campaign from existing for many years. Much of the information on the campaign can be found on http s://stanstedairportwatch.com and I am grateful to Brian Ross, the Chairman of the campaign, for allowing me to use the materials and summarise the background to the campaign.

The group, Stansted Airport Watch (SAW) has around 7,500 members and registered online supporters including about 150 special interest and environmental organisations, parish and town councils and other communities who feel that they are threatened by expansion of the airport.

The original campaign began life as the North West Essex and East Herts Preservation Association ('NWEEHPA') in 1965. In 2002, the government published proposals for expanding airport capacity in the UK and Stansted was a main focus. The proposal included the expansion of Stansted by adding as many as three additional runways, which would have made Stansted twice the size of Heathrow.

A working group, Stop Stansted Expansion (SSE), was established to resist the proposals and an open invitation was made to local organisations (such as Friends of the Earth, CPRE and others) and individuals to help form a campaign group to oppose the expansion.

At the outset, it was recognised that the Working Group needed to consider all matters relating to the operation and development of Stansted Airport in the context of sustainable development. It would need to conduct or commission research; increase public awareness of the issues; liaise with other organisations; conduct campaigns; and make representations to government departments, local authorities and other relevant bodies.

NWEEHPA itself became SAW in May 2021, with SSE put into hibernation in case major expansion was proposed again.

As the group says:

> we have resolved to use all lawful measures necessary to achieve our objective including:

- Pursuing our vigorous campaign of publicity, lobbying and grass roots activities.
- Increasing public awareness of the issues in order to gain support.
- Making representations to government departments, local authorities, the City and other decision-makers and influencers.
- Identifying and, where necessary, pursuing legal challenges.
- Challenging inappropriate expansion proposals for Stansted Airport via the planning system.
- Conducting and commissioning inquiries and research to support the campaign.
- Building partnerships with like-minded organisations based on common ground.[4]

Their activities are supported through communications, events and a range of other actions.

The group's progress

At their time of the group's launch in 2002, whilst three additional runways were not expected, one certainly was. This was confirmed the following year in the government's Air Transport White Paper.

The then Aviation Minister informed SSE that it would have been more than one runway had it not been for the strength of the campaign they had organised. However, they expected the group to settle for this 'compromise' and give up their campaign.

But convinced that the economic case for expansion was weak and concerned about the environmental threat, they kept the campaign going.

In May 2010, the government withdrew its support for any major expansion of Stansted and the planning application for a second runway was withdrawn.

However, the threat re-emerged in September 2012 when the government established the Airports Commission with the task of examining whether the UK needed new runway capacity and, if so, where this should be built. The Commission concluded in December 2013 that at least one new runway would be needed in the Southeast by 2030.

The campaign engaged fully with the Airports Commission and succeeded in keeping Stansted off the Commission's shortlist of new runway options.

The campaign though continues to remind government, local politicians, the media and others that there is no justification for major expansion at Stansted.

How it secured achievements

The group works with other airport community groups and environmental NGOs, for example by lobbying for an end to the aviation industry's blanket exemption from fuel duty and VAT.

But the heart of the effectiveness of the group is its membership and supporters. 'The support of our volunteer team and the backing of so many in the community – from individuals to elected representatives, Parliamentarians to other environmental groups – has been key to our effectiveness of SSE over the years'.[5]

The actions of the group have included:

- a successful High Court challenge against the 2002 government consultation on developing new airport capacity in the southeast, forcing a re-run of the consultation
- a legal challenge of the 2003 Air Transport White Paper and forcing a new consultation on runway siting options
- opposing the cross-subsidy of Stansted by more profitable BAA (the former owners) airports helped persuade the economic regulator (the CAA) to prohibit cross-subsidisation, thereby reducing the financial viability of expansion at Stansted
- made a contribution to the break-up of the BAA monopoly by bringing the issue to the fore in the media, in Westminster, Whitehall, Brussels, at BAA AGMs, through unusual collaboration with certain airlines and shareholders and by extensive evidence to the Monopolies Commission (now the Competition and Markets Authority)
- Parliamentary action to secure amendments to the Civil Aviation Bill 2006 to force the government to retain numerical limits on night flights at Stansted
- lobbying for an increase in Air Passenger Duty
- nine separate evidence submissions to the Airports Commission and launching legal proceedings against it forcing the resignation of one of its members, because they were concerned about a potential conflict of interest.

The campaign has always used well-researched facts and has worked with like-minded campaign groups, emphasising the need to build relationships and trust with politicians, civil servants, opinion formers and the media – locally and nationally. Their current priorities of the group are:

- to ensure that the Government, local politicians, the media and others are constantly reminded that there is no justification for major expansion at Stansted.
- to maintain pressure on Stansted Airport to minimise the day-to-day (and night-to-night) impact of its operations on the local community.
- to work with other airport community groups and environmental NGOs, to continue to press for action to tackle the growing impact of aviation on climate change, for example by lobbying for a moratorium on airport expansion, legally binding limits on aviation greenhouse gas emissions and an end to the aviation industry's blanket exemption from fuel duty and VAT.
- to persuade Stansted Airport to sell back into private ownership the remainder of the local homes bought in connection with its earlier major expansion plans.[6]

The campaign's team of volunteers continue to work on a wide-reaching programme of activities, at community level and in specialist areas. The 'Take Action' section of the campaign's website shows how important they are to the success of its work. It provides a clear understanding of what supporters can do themselves. It includes membership, making a donation but also practical steps such as reporting noisy aircraft, getting others involved, writing to the press and attending events.

What can we take from this campaign?

There is no doubting the success delivered by the campaign. What a motivated group can achieve over a long period of time is a lesson not only to similar groups but also to the businesses that can find themselves on the receiving end of such a campaign.

If a business is going to propose a project or similar form of activity, locally or nationally, then it has to appreciate what is likely to come their way, the time and effort involved and the commitment necessary on their part. This is one reason why, it would appear, the current owners of the airport make the strong commitment that they do about wanting to be a trusted neighbour.

Yet once lost, or never achieved in the first place, trust is difficult to establish or recover. Many audiences may be sceptical from the outset, but actions are critical. Actions designed to build trust can have a positive outcome. Actions that do not consider the importance of building trust will entrench views.

It could be suggested that the response to the SSE campaign was mixed. The campaign received huge support from local residents and environmental groups but also faced opposition from business groups and some politicians who argued that the expansion was necessary for economic growth and job creation.

But that is to miss the point. The campaign was successful in preventing the expansion of the airport and any campaign that believes it can always carry all audiences with them is starting off on the wrong foot. There will always be audiences to manage and those that fundamentally disagree with you. The campaign strategy has to recognise that, manage audiences, engage where possible and argue against in other circumstances.

If everyone agreed, then a campaign would not have been needed.

There are a number of lessons that can be taken from the campaign around Stansted:

- Maintain momentum over time – recognising that a campaign has different stages of activity.
- Supply regular updates and engagement with activists – keeping your supporters engaged and involved means being the key trusted source of information and getting it to them promptly.
- Show local communities how they can get involved easily and with minimal effort but provide a range of options for those who want to be more active and involved. Give something for everyone.
- Make campaigning materials readily available to empower supporters. Materials need to provide facts that can be utilised but ideally in a range of formats which suit the activist but also the intended audience as well.
- Allow space for support in kind – communities could well have a range of skills and experience that can be utilised in a campaign: legal, communications, media relations, planning, finance etc. Give them all a chance to contribute.
- Recognise the power and value of the personal commitment involved – never taking that for granted.
- Do not underestimate the need for finance – in this case that could be used in legal challenges.
- Understand all aspects of the decision-making process locally and nationally.

None of this is to say that companies cannot be highly motivated, but the reality is that in any company people move on, new teams come in, company commitments can change over time, information can be lost, new priorities take over. In contrast, a community can retain a laser-like focus, as for them the campaign will be personal.

I discussed how best to develop build relationships with communities when looking to develop a new project with Graham Olver, a strategic and commercial leader with over 30 years' international business and project experience.

He pointed to the need to secure multiple points of engagement, through community leaders, whilst also recognising the many types and forms of community that will be impacted by a project. This includes those directly and indirectly affected and beneficiaries, faith groups and those outside the mainstream. There is often a need to reflect different languages and culturally appropriate connections as well as using channels such as social media to work with a younger generation.

When it comes to ensuring that loud voices do not dominate, Graham suggested securing multiple ways to get feedback and looking beyond statutory requirements. This can mean redesigning off-putting forms and developing better questions.

Internally, ensuring that community / activist voices are considered and responded to means, for Graham, disciplined recording and analysis allowing for accurate and comprehensive responses.

Graham's key pieces of advice for those developing projects about engaging with communities is to 'design to engage'. He believes that consultants seem to want to minimise responses as that means there are fewer to handle. It is important to use lessons from behavioural sciences and web / social media methods to keep attention and gamify.

The tactics employed by community groups / activists can occupy a huge amount of time and financial resources for a project. Graham believes that this can be best managed through authentic engagement. 'Do it well', he suggests, 'and become a human connection. Get to know them. Let them see that you are trying to be fair and responsible and that you are challenging yourselves to improve and not just tick boxes'.

Graham believes that it is important to always be engaging internally as well as it has purpose and value and should never feel like ticking a box.

He also provides a list of other issues that should be considered:

- Find the quest.
- Compete on storytelling.
- Invest in feedback loops.
- Maintain high energy.
- Active listening.
- Be prepared to change.
- Target those who benefit.
- Always have something to give to the protestors.
- Engage with all forms of media and debate.
- Invest in community enabling projects.
- Don't bullshit or greenwash.

Business and communities working together

There are some very good examples of businesses involved in major infrastructure projects working together with communities.

I spoke to Tom McGarry who has been involved in projects and community relations for many years. He works for Strategic Infrastructure, National Grid but prior to this he was responsible for the public consultation on EDF's Sizewell C Project from 2010–2023.

We started our discussion by considering the steps he has taken to build relationships with communities and keep them engaged over time.

> The critical aspect was to get out there and meet people as early as possible. When you know you have a major development coming forward it is important to meet local residents and representatives and answer their immediate questions and queries before you start the consultation process. If the Parish Council chair or a neighbour have a name and a face for the project, that is useful for them and an opportunity to build trust and work together on elements of the project or process. They may be for it or against it, but we aimed to get off on a constructive and positive foot.
>
> We asked local communities in focus groups what forms of communication they preferred. The answer was unequivocally that newsletters through the post, posters on the village notice boards and face-to-face meetings were appreciated far more than social media or websites. We were not too surprised given the demographics, but it was important to have this confirmed.
>
> From there on in, major project news was communicated via newsletter and press releases. They averaged three or four a year. We had a dedicated place to meet people. The Sizewell C Information Office on Leiston High Street opened its doors to the public on 21 November 2012 – the first day of Stage 1 consultation. However there had already been several meetings with local community groups and parishes before then. After the opening of the office, hundreds of people came through the door to ask about Sizewell C. We established a freephone community line and email address and always honoured a commitment to respond to queries within five working days.
>
> We continued to offer regular meetings to local parish councils and built strategic partnerships with key organisations in Suffolk so we could progress skills, employment and supply chain opportunities ahead of potential development consent. This helped to answer the challenge 'what's in it for me?'
>
> My personal commitment, I lived in Suffolk, meant that I could devote the necessary resources, time, energy and attention to detail that a project of this scale requires.

Working out who the key communities to engage with were was a challenge but Tom suggested that for Nationally Significant Infrastructure Projects it is important to understand the whole life cycle of the project.

> We need to identify the likely issues which would arise from the impact of construction, such as increases in traffic, changes to the landscape, the social impacts of a transient workforce and so on.

Nuclear Power Stations are quiet places once in operation, but they take a long time to build with a lot of people involved, and construction involves millions of tonnes of steel and concrete. It is not just the community immediately near the building site which is affected. There are several communities on the main roads and rail line to the construction area that will experience disruption. We had to consider the needs of all these communities.

Locally, and further afield, there are hundreds of people who would benefit from the opportunities presented by the Project.

For Tom, the key steps to identifying the Project's stakeholders were:

- Identifying the issues arising from construction (good and bad) with the Project Team and mapping them across the local area.
- Undertaking research (a community and political audit) to identify local leaders, representatives, clubs, schools, colleges and so on in those areas. The more local the better, which involves going to the parish level where possible and working from there.
- Meeting people early and making sure you are well briefed on their interests and concerns.
- Always remember there is no one, big homogenous community. Always think in the plural. There are communities. They all have different views and responses.
- Engaging in active and deep listening while always remembering that listening is not the same as agreeing. It is the responsibility of developers to show they have listened by explaining why things have changed as a result. But equally, they may have to explain why some things have had to remain as originally proposed. The important thing is to properly address the questions, not to ignore them.
- Always try and maintain a constructive relationship with the local authorities. They want your consultation to be well run and succeed because they are accountable to the local communities you are working with. They have experience and knowledge you can draw on, so if you are unsure about who to see, then ask the local authority. Crucially, there are key documents, such as a Statement of Community Consultation, that should never be submitted without having discussed it with them first. Otherwise, you will just look ill-informed, and it will set the project back.

As Tom detailed, one of the key challenges in working with a local community is ensuring that their feedback is considered and responded to. On some occasions changes will be made. On others, the project team may decide that no change is possible. This means there is always a challenge in ensuring that a project team properly listens and responds to community feedback. When discussing how this could be achieved, Tom noted that he was in a fortunate position for his project.

> There was a very positive internal culture in EDF and the Hinkley and Sizewell projects which really did prioritise community feedback. The proof of that was how much the Sizewell C project developed over time, reflecting the feedback received from stakeholders. It was also shown in a Report on Consultation that reached about 16 volumes in the end. This was because it was a qualitative exercise addressing every single issue raised in the consultation, rather than simply a numbers-focused quantitative one that just noted the numbers of who turned up and indicated a site preference.

> We wanted to make sure people found the consultation as accessible and useful as possible, so we also commissioned independent market research to ask people what they thought as they left public exhibitions. As a result, each time we held a consultation it was improved upon.

> As I noted above, while often robust the relationship with the county and district councils was constructive. EDF and local councils actively shared and discussed feedback from local communities. The result was that the feedback was then discussed and negotiated with planners and councillors and there were changes to the proposals. As a result, the application for a Development Consent Order to build Sizewell C which was submitted in May 2020 was a very different project from the initial proposals presented in November 2012. This process also informed the Deed of Obligation (financial commitments to the local communities and environment).

> While the adequacy of consultation test, the requirements to demonstrate sufficient consultation with stakeholders, may not be a high bar it is still an important one and it is necessary to demonstrate you have met your commitments to the Planning Inspectorate.

There were though, of course, community groups who expressed major issues of disagreement with the proposals for such a sizeable project, not least because it would involve a decade of construction. There were people who were 'upset and angry'. As Tom recalls:

> At one particular event there was a parish council that promised a meeting with me but turned it into a public meeting of 200 people all there to vent. It was focused on the 'park and ride' site and of course, the meeting was a disaster for all concerned. It became an opportunity for those who organised it to whip up anger. However, I had half expected it and I showed a slide that outlined how much effort we had gone to engage with the parish council and local residents. There was also the promise of further consultation and changes. And about half the room was decidedly happier

when they heard it would not be used as a lorry park, only as a temporary park and ride site for local workers.

Those one-off instances can be managed. Just as inevitable as they are, the formation of organised protest groups is also likely. The important thing to do is to treat all stakeholders equally, including those against the project. They were invited into the consultative Community Forum and engaged with throughout consultations.

Tom provided these key pieces of advice about engaging with communities for those developing projects.

- If in doubt about who to meet, seek advice from the local authorities and planners and get their advice.
- Make sure you know the area inside out. If you're not local, then stay there for a while and drive and walk around the place. You have no business consulting on proposals if you don't know the entire area.
- Identify your local representatives, landowners, neighbours and residents and start engaging with them as early as possible in the process.
- Always do your best to be available to these groups.
- Always listen carefully. Listening may not be the same as agreeing but often local residents have great ideas that can improve development proposals and help to make them work better for the community.
- Always give straight answers. No respect or mutual trust can be built out of waffle or spin.
- Keep the lines of communication open throughout the entire process and beyond.
- Don't be tempted to do everything via Teams or Zoom. They are useful tools and were especially vital during lockdown – but nothing is better than turning up and meeting face-to-face.

Diverse communities

Communities though can come in many shapes and forms. As a well as a 'local' community of the type described above, it is also possible to have communities of like-minded people, or those who represent, are from, a group in society. They too will campaign vigorously.

One such campaign is the Internet Watch Foundation (IWF) which exists 'to hunt down and remove any online record of child sexual abuse'.[7] I spoke to Michael Tunks, the IWF's now former Head of Policy and Public Affairs, about the challenges involved in running the campaign. It is an example of a campaign that works in partnership with the internet and tech industries, global law enforcement, governments, the education sector, charities and non-profits.

We started by considering the key factor (or factors) behind the formation of the Foundation.

In 1996, the Metropolitan Police identified indecent images of children on some UK based newsgroups and notified the Internet Service Providers Association. At the time, the police believed this may have constituted an offence under the 1978 Protection of Children Act, by the Internet Service Providers. The industry responded by trying to find a way to combat the hosting of this imagery, whilst protecting the tech community from being held criminally liable for providing access to the imagery. Put simply, something had to be done.

Discussions between the Department for Trade and Industry, Home Office, Metropolitan Police, some ISPs, and the Safety Net Foundation (formed by the Dawe Charitable Trust) then took place to discuss what potential solutions might be. Out of those discussions the Internet Service Providers Association the London Internet Exchange and Safety Net Foundation would create the R3 Safety Net Arrangement regarding rating, reporting and responsibility. An important element of the agreement was to establish an independent organisation to receive, assess and trace public complaints about child sexual abuse imagery on the internet and to support the development of specific website rating systems.

From that, the Internet Watch Foundation was born. Our hotline, which receives reports from members of the public of suspected child sexual abuse material, and back when it was formed also covered criminally obscene adult content, which has since been removed from our remit, opened in December 1996. Since then, we have had to adapt and develop rapidly to stay agile to changes in technology and the scale and threat that child sexual abuse imagery being shared online has significantly increased in the past 25 years.

I was interested in hearing how they balance the aims and values of the Foundation with the pressure applied by the public, government and other stakeholders on supporters:

> The IWF is an independent not-for-profit organisation and is governed by an independent board of 11 Trustees. We have representation from the technology industry, experts in human rights, law enforcement, safeguarding, legal and finance professionals that make up that Board and they are responsible for ensuring the good governance of the Foundation in line with the expectations set out in charitable law, alongside our Senior Leadership Team.
>
> We are, however, a unique organisation in that we also have several checks and balances, which ensure a healthy tension is embedded in the work that we do. We are independent of government and law enforcement, but it is vitally important we have good relationships with both. We have a Memorandum of Understanding with the National Police Chiefs' Council and Crown Prosecution Service that governs our operations and ensures that our analysts are free from prosecution when

carrying out their work, as assessing illegal child sexual abuse material is obviously a crime. We also work very closely with the Home Office's Child Abuse Image Database as a trusted vote within that system and are the only non-law-enforcement agency to have access to this database.

We also need the support of industry. We are a membership-based organisation, and we have a sliding scale of fees based on the size, sector, and number of employees a company has, which determines how much they pay to be a member of the IWF. The very largest members such as Meta, Apple, Google, Amazon, Microsoft will pay £80,000 per year to access the technical services that we provide to help keep their platforms free from child sexual abuse material, and the very smallest ones, the long tail of tech, pay as little as £1,000 per year. This means that small SMEs have access to the same level of service as some of the very largest players in the market. All of the funding we receive goes directly back into further developing and enhancing our response to tackling child sexual abuse online.

Industry also play an important role in the removal of child sexual abuse material. The IWF is the recognised body for Notice and Takedown in the UK, and once companies are notified that they are hosting illegal content, they are required to remove it under the terms of the European Union's e-commerce directive. The fastest time for removal is in under two minutes, thanks to the strong working relationship that IWF has with industry partners. The UK hosts very little of this content now. Ever since 2003, less than 1% of the content we have actioned for removal has been found hosted in the UK, meaning most of the content we request for removal is hosted extraterritorially, mainly in Europe, which in 2022 accounted for 66% of all the content we removed from the internet.

Our core purpose has always been the protection of children and our mission is to eradicate child sexual abuse material online. These are the core principles that guide us in the work that we do and in how we balance the competing views of stakeholders. Alongside the important relationships we have with government, law enforcement, and industry, we also run public awareness campaigns to inform the public of the scale and nature of child sexual abuse and how it manifests online. We have run campaigns warning parents of the sheer scale of offenders there are in the UK, we have empowered young girls to block, report and tell someone they trust if they are approached by strangers online, we have encouraged members of the public to report to us and know the law if they stumble across what they suspect might be child sexual abuse online and have also warned of changes in technology which make these images and videos much harder to detect. In terms of our advocacy efforts, we have always sought to be a balanced and sensible voice in discussions that has sought to draw together and convene views of industry, government and law enforcement to ensure that we have laws that are practical, fit for purpose and technically viable.

We discussed how the IWF builds support with stakeholders, such as government, in the face of potential scepticism about links with the industry. A challenge that could easily face other activist groups.

> The view of the IWF amongst political stakeholders is a positive one. We are viewed as an organisation that exists for public benefit and that wants to do all that we can to eradicate child sexual abuse online, and the issue of our industry funding is rarely mentioned. If it does come up, we are able to point to a demonstrable track record over the past 25 years of tackling child sexual abuse and making the UK one of the most hostile places in the world to host child sexual abuse material. We are held up as the 'gold standard' across the world with how we tackle this issue, by the INHOPE association of internet hotlines.
>
> We also point to our independence and the quality of our data. In analysing whether a piece of content is illegal or not we are guided by the Sentencing Council Guidelines (2014) and our judgments are completely free from industry involvement. Our analysts are highly trained, deeply knowledgeable and their judgement is trusted by law enforcement. The quality of the data we provide to industry and to law enforcement demonstrates that we are a strong partner in the fight against the spread of child sexual abuse online and really underpins all our relationships, whether that is with government, law enforcement or industry. Without strong, quality-assured data, we would not be able to build trust and confidence in how we are governed.
>
> We also have strong safeguards in place. In 2014 we carried out a Human Rights review of our organisation, with a former Director General of Public Prosecutions, Lord Ken Macdonald. We implemented his review in full and published the review on our website, which further built trust and confidence in us as an organisation.
>
> In March 2020, the Independent Inquiry into Child Sexual Abuse concluded: 'We were a large part of the reason comparatively little child sexual abuse material is hosted in the UK and we are an organisation which deserves to be publicly acknowledged as such'.
>
> We also highlight other similar models of best practice in other sectors and industries. For example, the way IWF operates has similarities with advertising industry.

I asked whether some tactics / approaches work better than others:

> We have often found that if we are able to get government ministers to visit our organisation, the more they begin to understand our work, how we operate and the impact that we have.
>
> One of the popular parts of any visit is getting Ministers to speak to our analysts, the people that are removing this content and viewing it

daily. We often find that them describing what is happening in the images, how we must work to remove this and some of their frustrations and motivations for doing the job they do, often comes across really well.

The IWF also runs a Parliamentary Champions programme. This gives parliamentarians an opportunity of becoming regularly involved with our work, receive updates and running promotional material on their Twitter accounts, which naturally leads to further questions, regular engagement and also helps in pushing our policy messages with government.

We also take a collaborative approach and often convene discussions between government, law enforcement and industry as key legislative initiatives or issues develop.

When it came to common misunderstandings that have to be overcome, Michael said:

Some of the main misunderstandings we have to overcome are often related to how the technology industry works, operates and responds to changes in regulation. Amongst some Parliamentarians there is an extremely strong understanding of the industry, some have worked in industry and understand it extremely well, but they are by and large in the minority amongst the wider group in Parliament.

The challenge as always for public affairs and policy professionals is trying to distil an incredibly complex topic into a 30-minute conversation or a two-page briefing note. Often politicians' focus tends to be on some of the largest platforms and providers, because they know them and media attention is diverted in that direction, but quite often it is small platforms or image hosting boards or cyberlockers which many people have never heard of that are responsible for hosting the majority of this content on the open internet.

It is often also tricky to explain what companies do now against the backdrop of a political narrative that they are failing. There are distinct nuances, for example, in platform reporting and transparency. Some send millions of reports to the US National Center for Missing and Exploited Children, but are these found before they are uploaded? After they are uploaded? How long have they stayed live for? Others send very few.

We ended by discussing what would be considered success.

At the moment, there are two different pieces of legislation that may have some impact on the IWF. This includes the UK's Online Safety Bill and the European Union's new proposal: Laying down rules to prevent and combat child sexual abuse material.

In the UK, we have been working hard to get the Bill onto the statute books. We believe that it could make a difference in improving the response to the spread of this content online, but we have to be clear that it will not be a silver bullet. There is not one single solution to solving the problem of child sexual abuse online. After the Online Safety Bill receives Royal Assent, we will need to ensure there is recognition of the IWF's role in helping deliver the regulation and ensuring companies are well equipped to respond to their new regulatory responsibilities.

But we will also need to look at what comes next. We need effective prevention campaigns to discourage the creation of this imagery in the first place, we will need closer collaborative working with other countries as this is a global problem and we need to strengthen frameworks and collaboration internationally.

There is a lot still to be done and the fight will continue.

At IWF, we will continue to strengthen our approach and partnerships with government, industry, law enforcement and regulators to improve the technological response to this issue. Ultimately, we want to see a world where we are reducing the amount of material we are removing from the internet, because there is less of it out there, but due to changes in technology, we need to be careful that increased regulation means that we are not simply pushing the problems into corners of the internet where it is harder to detect, find and take down.

Reflections

It is clear that campaigners are motivated and the more personal an issue, the more motivated they can be. Local communities are an excellent example of this type of motivated audience.

Their importance is obviously most keenly felt in the shaping and the outcomes of projects and development plans. Considering these reveals that:

- Even if a community lacks financial resources, they will find other ways to mobilise themselves through expert networks, social media, and political advocacy to exert influence.
- Early and meaningful engagement with an audience is crucial. When businesses fail to consider an audience's needs or interests from the outset then they risk antagonising them which, in turn, increases the prospect of facing opposition. An early emphasis on communication, relationship-building, dialogue and listening are critical in avoiding protracted conflicts.
- A community's power can grow over time. Businesses need to appreciate that activism can be sustained over decades, learning from past experiences. Both activists and businesses must prepare for long-term campaigns and evolving strategies.

The local context shows businesses that a proactive, collaborative approach, based on the needs of that community, is the only way forward. That understanding of an audience, built through a variety of means, is always of value. Investing in genuine, ongoing engagement; being flexible following input; and adapting to changing circumstances are all part of those efforts. That requires resources being committed from the outset so that trust can be built but also the whole organisation recognising and being committed to change, if demanded and feasible. Compromise is not a dirty word or a sign of weak leadership but an outcome of working together.

Communities should never take their position for granted. They can certainly wield power and influence when organised, but unrealistic expectations can risk support and can provide businesses with an opportunity to undermine them. The community support could fracture, diminish and leave businesses free to ignore even the most sensible of requests.

Constructive engagement can only be achieved if businesses and communities actively look for ways to work together. In that way a sustainable solution can be developed.

Notes

1 Copper Consultancy, 'Past, present, future: The infrastructure lifecycle from the perspective of communities', November 2022, https://copperconsultancy.com/wp-content/uploads/2022/11/Past-Present-and-Future-The-infrastructure-lifecycle-from-the-perspective-of-communities.pdf
2 Copper Consultancy, 'Past, present, future: The infrastructure lifecycle from the perspective of communities', November 2022, https://copperconsultancy.com/wp-content/uploads/2022/11/Past-Present-and-Future-The-infrastructure-lifecycle-from-the-perspective-of-communities.pdf
3 Stansted Airport website, www.stanstedairport.com/community/
4 Stansted Airport Watch website, https://stanstedairportwatch.com/about-us/what-we-do/
5 Stansted Airport Watch website, https://stanstedairportwatch.com/about-us/achievements-to-date/
6 Stansted Airport Watch website, https://stanstedairportwatch.com/the-threat/our-current-priorities/
7 Internet Watch Foundation, www.iwf.org.uk/about-us/why-we-exist/

Chapter 3

Business relations

Many organisations focus on their external profile believing that having a strong brand and reputation will help them deal with most issues. Stakeholders will work with them, and it also insulates the organisation if things go wrong.

But the reality is that demands made of an organisation by those they employ can be the most powerful voice of all. Other stakeholders always listen to those from within the organisation. Many believe that it exposes the reality of an organisation. That can be both positive and negative. Employees are the best champions, but they are also the worst enemies to make.

People listen and that makes what employees say, and how they behave, significant.

The organised reality

The power of organised labour has traditionally been wielded by trade unions. This, of course, varies between countries but the use of a collective voice to demand and secure change is a well-trodden path. Thanks to such collective action, organisations have been forced to improve wages, working conditions, opportunities for progression and the list goes on. Some trade unions are plugged into politics as well either directly through involvement in political parties or as de facto lobbyists pushing for legislative or regulatory change.

Organised action by employees is nothing new but businesses have increasingly witnessed campaigns from within their own ranks from individuals and smaller groups. Most notably this has been happening within companies that have tried their best to avoid encouraging trade union activity. The tech sector, whose larger players have often come from the US, have always contended that they look after their employees and that there is no need for any organised, collective actions.

But in some high-profile cases, employees have come together in an attempt to force changes on these business operations, in circumstances not normally associated with organised collective action.

DOI: 10.4324/9781003371908-4

The reality is that any organisation, whether they work closely with organised internal groups or not, still need to have ways of listening and engaging with their employees.

The operational reality is that any organisation needs to have channels open. It needs to listen and respond.

The drivers of actions by employees have various roots but often arise from:

- a deep frustration with the behaviour and actions of an organisation which is being ignored
- the deliberate exclusion of views
- a gap, which they are aware of, between the external statements of an organisation and its actual operations
- a consistent failure to deliver which others are unaware of
- a consistent failure to deliver which others are failing to highlight
- deliberate attempts to disguise behaviour or actions, in other words engaging in a 'cover-up'.

But rather than always being viewed as a negative, employee activism can be viewed as a valuable source of information and can be used to strengthen operations and reputations. Too often though, it is seen as reputationally damaging, and the immediate focus is on what could happen to the bottom line.

But the expectations of employees have changed. A survey from LinkedIn showed that workers, especially younger one, expect their employers to abide by values. More than two-thirds (68%) of professionals in Europe want to work for companies that share their values with nearly 9 in 10 Gen Zers and Millennials saying they would leave a job to work somewhere that better matches their values.[1]

The challenge to attract the best talent, especially from the younger generations, is therefore at least in part about having values and living by them. In turn though that increases the prospects of being called out for not having values or having values that are not delivered on. There is though potentially a huge bonus for those who have the values and deliver on them.

The most dangerous situation for any organisation is where the gap exists.

When workers stand up

One of the most high-profile, and successful, examples of employee activism has happened at Apple.

Janneke Parrish is an organiser, activist and co-founder of Apple Together who provided me with some fascinating details about the campaign. It describes itself as 'a global solidarity union made up of workers from all parts of Apple organizing for a say in our workplace'.[2]

On its website, it points out that:

Apple prides itself on its commitment to diversity, equity, and an environment where everyone can do their best work. But Apple has fallen short of this goal for so many of our current and former team-mates, so we made space to share those stories with #AppleToo.[3]

Janneke Parrish (Apple Together)

In spring of 2021, the tech giant, Apple, prepared to emerge from the Covid-19 pandemic. Through public health initiatives throughout the United States and increased vaccination rates around the world, the number of Covid-19 cases had fallen to lows not seen since the start of the pandemic. For many, this heralded the impending end of the pandemic and a return to the normalcy so many yearned for.

For Apple, the decline in the number of cases and end of the pandemic meant something more. It meant that its time of having nearly all of its corporate workforce working remotely was ending. Apple workers would be returning to their offices.

Prior to the pandemic, Apple had not been remote work friendly. It prided itself on its culture of collaboration, and the idea that two people meeting and chatting face-to-face were what fuelled its culture of innovation. It was in these serendipitous moments that could only happen between those working in a common space that had led to its status as one of the world's largest tech companies. Apple had invested heavily in its offices, especially in California and Texas, creating office spaces that were landmarks in their communities, replete with every amenity a tech worker could need. In-office work lay at the core of Apple's culture and, in the view of its leadership, its success.

However, these offices masked a darker reality for the workers within them. For those in California, housing prices in the Bay Area meant many faced hours-long commutes every day, and agonising decisions about how to divide their time between their families and their jobs. The offices themselves were so crowded that being able to book a meeting room sometimes meant traveling across mul-tiple campuses to be able to have the coveted face-to-face meetings. Apple Park with its distinctive circular shape was nightmarish for the teams working within it to navigate, having dedicated its space to make it easy for executives to see teams working, but giving little space to the teams to actually do their work.

For those in Austin TX, depending on the team they were part of, the focus on in-person work meant career opportunities were limited unless a person was willing to move to California. Though its housing market was cheaper, Austin was less well-designed to handle the large amounts of traffic its exploding growth brought, and so commutes could still be hours long. The Austin campus, too, was overcrowded, and with fewer opportunities to engage in the perks that Apple prided itself on for its workers.

Remote work, on paper, should have resolved some of these issues. Allowing workers to work remotely would have reduced overcrowding, ended long commutes, and made career and networking opportunities accessible to everyone, regardless of their campus. However, Apple resisted, instead focusing on the idea that its culture only succeeded because of physical proximity.

This idea was put to the test by the Covid-19 pandemic. In March 2020, Apple shut down its offices and sent nearly all of its workers home to work remotely for the duration of the pandemic. An unintentional experiment in whether Apple could continue to succeed with its workers remote had begun.

The experiment was a resounding success.

Throughout the company, teams not only continued the same quality of work, but in many cases, exceeded their goals, spurring initiatives at an unheard-of pace. Workers were more productive than ever. For many, working remotely also presented the opportunity to improve their work-life balance, allowing them to focus on their families, their hobbies and their health. Workers in remote sites were now able to participate in events that had previously only been accessible to those in California, and the introduction of a universal chat platform across the company brought workers from every corner of the company together. The culture that Apple had prided itself on, of collaboration and serendipitous meetings, was alive and well, and perhaps stronger than it had ever been by virtue of the new forums in which these meetings and discussions could take place. Many workers expected that, after seeing how productive and happy workers could be while working remotely, Apple would reconsider its stance on remote work and allow workers to decide for themselves where they would work.

In spring 2021, it became clear that would not be the case. Everyone, regardless of their productivity, the benefits to their health, or their work-life balance, would be expected to return to offices in the coming summer.

Prior to this point, when Apple leadership made a decision, workers had little choice but to abide by it. Apple's culture of silence and siloing, and the physical separation between workers, made it difficult, if not impossible, to organise around issues. However, working from home and communicating via Slack changed everything. Workers were no longer siloed or isolated. Rather, workers from around the world were able, via Slack, to strategise and organise around the issues that mattered to them.

Organisers got to work, drafting an open letter and collecting anecdotes from their fellow workers, hoping that the sincerity of their convictions and strength of their arguments would convince Apple leadership to continue allowing them to work from home. Their optimism in the idea that an open letter and pressure from workers could make a difference wasn't misplaced – weeks earlier, an open letter and pressure from workers across the company had led to the firing of Antonio Garcia Martinez, a senior manager for the App Store.

A dozen organisers wrote the remote work open letter and gathered hundreds of signatures. In June 2021, the letter was submitted to Apple leadership. Its argument was simple – workers did their best work when they were happy and healthy, and many Apple workers were at their happiest and healthiest when working remotely.

The reply from Apple leadership came quickly. In a video from Deirdre O'Brien, Apple's head of the People team, Apple leadership dismissed the organisers' concerns. Apple's best work, O'Brien reiterated, could only be done in person and in offices. Any issues workers had within their teams were isolated incidents and should be discussed with managers. Concerns workers had about Covid were moot, as the pandemic was ending, and the severity of Covid was overblown. Workers and their concerns were dismissed.

Rather than be stymied, workers continued to push for remote work, restructuring their arguments to directly counter what leadership was telling them. Workers also began reaching out to other organisers, working on separate causes. Parallel to remote work advocacy, other workers at Apple had been investigating pay equity and coming to the conclusion that Apple paid men and women differently for equal work. Their activism followed the same familiar pattern – first engaging in good faith with leadership, having their concerns rebuffed or suppressed, and coming to the conclusion that Apple leadership had no intention of engaging in good faith. The two groups merged, coalescing what had been separate concerns under one over-arching umbrella – Apple and its culture of silence needed to change. Workers' voices needed to be heard.

AppleToo was born.

While many organisers continued to keep their advocacy internal, others chose to go public with their experiences, both in their careers at Apple, and in trying to advocate for change. Ashley Gjovik went public with her experiences of a toxic and sexist workplace, as well as concerns about environmental toxins in Apple offices. Cher Scarlett went public with her work on pay equity, being featured in the *Washington Post* and other publications, detailing not only how Apple had a pay gap between men and women, but the steps Apple leadership had taken to keep workers from discovering the gap. Janneke Parrish went public with her experiences of a toxic and sexist workplace and began sharing the stories that had been collected as part of the remote work advocacy movement, as well as additional stories that had been collected specifically as part of AppleToo.

These were not the first people to stand up to Apple, nor were they the last. However, with a surge of worker movements in 2021, their advocacy made headlines. AppleToo was one of several worker movements in the tech industry, part of a wave that seemed like it could reform the industry entirely.

For workers within Apple, though, seeing the attention that was paid to their normally hermit-like company was unprecedented. Apple's culture of silence was pervasive, in some cases convincing workers that even discussing their working conditions or wages with each other was a fireable offense. Seeing activists so publicly discussing their company and what it was like to work there opened the floodgates at Apple. More and more workers began to discuss their experiences, both internally and publicly, and joined the nascent AppleToo movement.

Though the organising had begun on Slack, concerns that conversations were being watched by leadership led organisers to move their conversations to Discord, another online chat platform. There, organisers planned what actions to take, where to focus their energy, and how to better organise. Intended or not, what had started as a push for individual causes had become a union organising committee.

Apple leadership responded, firing Ashley Gjovik and issuing a statement that those who spoke to external parties had no place at Apple. For the remaining organisers, this statement was a clear attempt to stifle organising and make it clear that continuing to organise presented a threat to their continued employment. The organisers took steps to protect themselves, including educating themselves and others on their rights and what to do if they faced termination.

The test of that preparation came days after the memo when one of the lead organisers was placed under investigation under suspicion of leaking confidential information. After two weeks of investigation, Janneke Parrish was fired, ostensibly for non-compliance with Apple's investigation. Parrish and AppleToo alleged that it was because of her work as an organiser.

Immediately following Parrish's firing, Parrish and the other organisers ensured that Apple's anti-organising actions became front page news. Every major US publication put the story front and centre. It spun its way internationally as well. Apple's actions against organisers exploded well beyond what Apple had anticipated, and in an instant, what had been a nascent movement became a bonfire.

Hundreds of workers, suddenly aware of what was happening, joined AppleToo, sharing their own stories and working together to plan next steps. Parrish filed an unfair labour practice charge against Apple, joining Gjovik and Scarlett in doing so. By the end of 2021, Apple appeared poised on a precipice, facing a surge of worker advocacy and a new age for workers' rights. Its future seemed analogous to Amazon's or Starbucks' – about to face a wave of unionising and worker advocacy.

The reality was different. On Christmas Eve 2021, workers in a Florida store, supported by Apple Together, staged a walkout. Throughout 2022, other stores filed union petitions, with two Apple stores ultimately succeeding in unionising. However, the wave of unions that Amazon and Starbucks had seen, and which seemed possible at the end of 2021, did not materialise. Apple successfully tamped down worker organising.

For those within AppleToo – now Apple Together – organising did not stop. Workers continued to organise, but faced an Apple that was better acclimated to their organising, and better prepared to stymie it. Apple changed its policies for Slack usage, for example, requiring vice president permission to create a new Slack channel. Stores attempting to unionise found themselves confronted by a law firm specialised in union busting, and strategies that used Apple's culture to further stymie attempts to unionise. Apple reiterated its culture as its key to why workers did not and should not organise, and it was effective.

The difficulties with organising through traditional pathways did not mean organising itself was ineffective. Much as Apple adapted after realising its union busting strategies were less than successful, Apple Together also adapted.

Rather than attempting to organise head-on, Apple Together used alternative strategies and used organisational structures themselves to achieve their ends.

During the 2021 shareholders' meeting, Nia Capital had put forward a proposal for a civil rights audit. The audit was based on the stories shared by AppleToo and Cher Scarlett's pay equity work and asked that Apple investigate whether all workers were being treated equally. This proposal passed, forcing Apple to conduct an internal audit. The collective actions by Apple workers had brought enough public scrutiny to sway Apple's shareholders.

AppleTogether saw this outcome and recognised the potential pathway before them. Rather than continuing internal pressure, AppleTogether drafted its own shareholder proposals, bringing the issues it saw with Apple's union-busting and return to office policies before both the Securities and Exchange Commission (SEC) and shareholders. The systems that had never traditionally been used for worker organising were now rife with opportunity to bring about change by appealing to the public and making workers' cases to the public at large. Though their 2022 proposals were not successful, the lesson had been learned – when it was not possible to make a difference internally, external avenues were still flush with opportunity. Moreover, 2023 and 2024 would see the National Labor Relations Board (NLRB) issue multiple charges against Apple on behalf of workers throughout both Apple's corporate and retail ecosystems, making it clear that the company was not above the law.

Throughout its work, AppleTogether has continued to grow, swelling from a dozen members to over a thousand. Its members continue to provide support to one another and continue to explore pathways to making change at one of the world's largest companies. It is this community of support that keeps them motivated, and the knowledge that every change, however small, is still the direct result of their collective action.

The example of Apple Together shows what can be achieved when motivated individuals focus on a campaign. That campaign can last a considerable period of time and is unlikely to really ever end.

Any campaign will elicit potentially contrasting views about whether its aims and actions are appropriate, acceptable, too costly, idealistic, or even counterproductive. The focus for the likes of Apple Together is very much on ensuring that a company lives by the values it sets. For other activist groups, the focus may be on trying to get the company to recognise and accept those values in the first instance.

This could mean that an organisation faces a continuum of activism (see Figure 3.1).

Figure 3.1 Continuum of activism

Value setting is placed in a wide context when activism focuses on societal change and looks to raise the profile of an issue. Think about all the campaigning work that has contributed to our understanding of the importance of addressing climate change.

Once the values have been set then there can be a focus on behaviour change. This could focus on communities but often targets larger organisations who play an important contributory role. In the case of climate change, the focus of activists could be on large-scale emitters. Over time there is a trickle down as the larger organisations change behaviour, then they can exert pressure on smaller organisations as will the activists themselves.

In the 'final' stage, the activists will maintain pressure to ensure that no gap emerges between the statement of the value and all aspects of its delivery.

Under this scenario it is a brave organisation that decides to wait until the activists start knocking at their door. It is always better to think ahead and change behaviour without being forced to do so.

Some may be genuinely committed to the change; others may simply do it to protect themselves and their organisations. To an extent, the motivation does not matter. What matters is the delivery.

Some organisations will stand firm and will not change. That is rarely a long-term strategy because stakeholders, often driven by the spotlight placed on an organisation by activists, will force change. Customers disappear or government changes laws or regulations to 'standardise' behaviour across a sector. Behavioural outliers rarely last long.

There are those organisations though that genuinely believe in a cause. We could think of that as being part of the 'value setting' stage. The companies themselves are almost part of the activist cause to seek wider change.

Apple is not alone in having been challenged by its employees.

The availability of online platforms has empowered voices. For instance, VFX artists have complained about how they are treated by Marvel.[4] Alphabet workers have similarly come together to form a union. Its mission states:

> Our union strives to protect Alphabet workers, our global society, and our world. We recognize our power as Alphabet workers – full-time employees, temporary employees, vendors, and contractors – comes from our solidarity with one another and our ability to collectively act to ensure that our workplace is equitable and Alphabet acts ethically.[5]

Not that any of this should have come as a shock to businesses. A 2019 Herbert Smith Freehills report looking at the future of work over the following 3–5 years found that:

- Over 80% of companies predicted a rise in workforce activism with 95% expecting an increase in workers' use of social media to amplify their voice.

- Respondents anticipated an increase in online digital petitions with 77% expecting to see more crowdfunded legal challenges.
- Workforce activism was seen to be a significant potential threat to corporate reputation.
- Almost 50% of respondents saw activism as a positive force for change.[6]

The examples of workplace activism are all around us, often daily. It is no surprise that leaders need help and support in reacting to the trend. Megan Reitz and John Higgins have written about the issues in 'Leading in an Age of Employee Activism',[7] and discussed the issues on the 'Dare to Lead with Brené Brown' podcast.[8]

Speaking at a TEDx Talk and based on the article, Megan Reitz suggested that:

- Activism is in the eye of the beholder – leaders need to understand the assumptions and judgements made by activists so that they can respond.
- Leaders can be detached from activist issues in an optimism bubble – the more senior a leader becomes, the most likely they are to overestimate their approachability and listening skills leading to an underestimation of their understanding of the strength of feeling of employees.
- You can't sit on the activism fence – inaction is as political as action. Leaders need to make authentic choices based on the views of stakeholders, including employees.
- Your response to activism has consequences – crucial amongst this is what employees think of the response. The response of leaders can take different forms, from suppression or legally led through to one that represents a step change and actively recruits and promotes activists.[9]

Concluding her talk, Reitz suggests that:

'Employee activism is not only here to stay, it is expected to become a defining feature of the workplace'.[10]

B-Corps

One way in which companies can clearly demonstrate their commitment to social and environment concerns, not just generate profits, is by achieving B-Corp certification. Some companies who achieve the certification may be seen as more activist than others, but they have all made a public commitment. Some are subsequently more vocal about it than others and some campaign on issues, others do not. There is no 'type' of B-Corp, each has their own personality and approach.

> Certified B Corporations are leaders in the global movement for an inclusive, equitable, and regenerative economy. Unlike other certifications for businesses, B Lab is unique in our ability to measure a company's entire social and environmental impact.[11]

Achieving the certification demonstrates a level of commitment and delivery. Some of the most well-known B-Corps include:

- Patagonia – the outdoor clothing and gear company long held up as an example of what businesses can achieve whilst not being focused solely on profits. This was further reinforced when its owner gave away its ownership and set up a trust structure so that all profits could be used to fight climate change. The company also has an activism section on its website to help support grassroots movements.
- Ben & Jerry's – the ice cream and frozen dessert company which often highlights issues of social justice.
- Divine Chocolate – the world's first and, so far only, Fairtrade and B-Corp certified premium chocolate company. The company has a particular focus on fighting exploitation in the cocoa industry.

The list of B-Corps continues to grow, and each company has its own reasons for signing up. But each one has to continue to maintain its standards and there are obvious reputational risks if these are not achieved.

That is also not to say that simply achieving B-Corp status is the end of the story. The certification scheme is not without its critics who have suggested the framework is not strong enough, that many of the companies who achieve the accreditation are still driven by profits, that it has become a business in itself to get new companies signed up, etc.

It can also be difficult to compare those who have signed up because there are different categories of companies. This means the amount of information provided to the public can vary.

Some critics argue that B-Corps do not provide enough information about their social and environmental impact, making it difficult to judge if they are truly committed to their mission of creating a positive impact.

In response to these types of criticisms, some have taken steps to increase transparency in their operations and reporting, for instance by publishing detailed impact reports. Others have put other standards and assessments in place alongside being a B-corp. All this is designed to further verify their social and environmental impact and assure stakeholders.

Some critics have pointed to the legal requirements not being as rigorous for B-Corps as they are for more traditional companies. If true, then that would open up the possibility of companies using the certification as a marketing tool. As a way of strengthening their reputation without having to really alter their ethos or actions.

There is an inbuilt tension in the nature of B-Corps. It is currently a way to help consumers make a choice based on their values. The more the number of companies achieving the accreditation increases, the less useful it becomes as such a 'short cut'.

Any standards process also runs the risk of not being able to force those who have already signed up to keep pushing the boundaries to improve. Another danger is that organisations put effort into achieving the standards rather than forcing themselves to actually change their behaviours.

Increasingly these types of criticisms have been addressed by law makers, companies and the B-Corp movement as a whole. It does not mean that anyone is immune from criticisms or that mistakes will not be possible in future, but properly policed it plays a useful role for stakeholders.

Whilst growing in number, B-Corps remain a very small percentage of the overall make-up of companies. That limits the change that is possible and the pace of change. However, this is being addressed by members as they work together on initiatives to have a wider impact on economies.

Whether the change B-Corps can achieve is radical enough is a further area of criticism. Some want to push radical and immediate change rather than the more incremental approach that they suggest B-Corps adopt.

It has to be remembered that B-Corps are all individual companies and can push progress at their own rates. Not many would accuse Patagonia of not being radical enough. But there are companies of all shapes, sizes and across many different sectors so they will not progress or challenge at the same rate.

Its rising numbers demonstrate that it is a useful driver of change.

However, achieving the status is not a panacea. Many B-Corps still get into trouble: BrewDog lost its status as a result of controversies about its work culture, Innocent Drinks fell foul of advertising standards and the signing up of Nespresso reawakened accusations of B-Corps as a form of greenwashing.

It is right that B-Corps are not immune to criticism or challenge, and they too can make mistakes just as any other business can. Despite the criticisms, many of which are being directly addressed, many B-Corps are widely praised for their commitment to social and environmental responsibility. They play a valuable role in showing the way for others.

Business activism

Many businesses have increasingly taken it upon themselves to be activists as well. Leading issues from the front. Being an activist company has become increasingly mainstream. Whilst Patagonia and Ben & Jerry's remain pre-eminent in most people's minds, others are unafraid to shy away from being seen as activists themselves.

Speaking on the Masters of Scale podcast, Peter McGuiness, the CEO of Impossible Foods, suggested that if you are running a values-based business that:

> You need to wade into societal things. You need to be a good corporate citizen.

But he drew a distinction between an activist brand and an active brand:

> I think my aspirations for Impossible is not to be an activist brand. It's to be an active brand. And so if you take a position on something that's important, and you piss a few people off along the way, they probably weren't the people that were going to buy your product anyway.
>
> We're not going to sit here and have a strong point of view on every single issue because I don't want to politicize this brand, and I don't want to make it into an activist brand, but we are going to wade into some certain things that we feel are very, very important. And that playbook is different for each company.[12]

In this reading, an activist brand is more political but that does not need to be the case. It may not be possible though to neatly divide the two. In some instances, the politicians themselves look to insert a dose of politics into the statements and actions of businesses.

In the same podcast series, Alexis McGill Johnson, President of Planned Parenthood, suggested that organisations such as hers are looking for companies to become more active on their issues.

'Every time a company stays neutral or tries to be a bystander, that's going to be to their detriment because their consumers care about this issue; their workforce is standing there. It's really important for them to show leadership in order to achieve many of their own values'.[13]

Part of their campaigning is to demonstrate how relevant their issue is to the company. In the case of Planned Parenthood:

> There are strong efforts, first and foremost, to protect their workforce, companies who are in states where their employees no longer have access to care, and they have made clear, full-throated decisions that they will continue to support the right to travel, as well as cover on insurance their care, and I think that's a good step.[14]

Of course, displaying and advocating values could alienate some, but those values are what drives the business, so its stakeholders expect them to be active. This is especially true of social issues. But there are issues that become important because of a mix of activist campaigns, changed public opinion or political interest (both soft, putting a spotlight on them; or hard, changed legislation, regulation of taxation).

Fundamentally though, companies can be active and be successful, whatever the measure they adopt for that is. American Express's former Chairman and CEO Ken Chenault quite clearly believes this: 'Corporations can be a force for good and they can also be very successful'.[15]

The pressure on companies to be more active comes through all elements of their organisation, not just their employees but their supply chain, the communities in which they operate and, not least, their consumers.

This could lead to Brand Activism that Philip Kotler and Christian Sarkar describe as consisting of:

> business efforts to promote, impede, or direct social, political, economic, and/or environmental reform or stasis with the desire to promote or impede improvements in society.[16]

There are some very good examples of brands delivering campaigns with a strong social message:

- Nike, 'For Once, Just Don't Do It', responding to the murder of George Floyd.
- Brewdog Forest, as part of its commitment to being the first carbon-negative global beer business.
- P&G supporting the empowerment of women and girls through the 'Like a Girl' campaign.

But there are also many examples of companies getting it chronically wrong as well, such as Amazon using a Black History Month campaign to include content from white creators.[17]

The *Financial Times'* Moral Money series cites Public Affairs Council research which showed that the level of pressure for corporate engagement in social issues is growing.[18] The Annenberg USC 2024 Global Communication Report points to more engagement by businesses in social movements. The title of a report from Quadriga University even recognises corporate activism as a 'rising trend'.[19]

Under those circumstances, how should companies react? The same *Financial Times* piece provides details of the five 'guidepost questions' used by IBM to help decide on which issues to engage:

- Is the issue directly linked to the business?
- Does the company have a history of engaging on it?
- What are the stakeholders (employees, clients and shareholders) saying?
- What are competitors doing?
- Could the company make a meaningful difference by engaging?[20]

Asking these sorts of questions helps to keep the activity authentic and explains why a business is being active. Business activism is not all positive.

I spoke to Lucy von Sturmer, the founder of award-winning impact consultancy The Humblebrag. A champion of business as a force for good, Lucy works to support business leaders and brands to take a stand on social, cultural and environmental issues. Lucy is also the initiator of Creatives for Climate, a global network of more than 30,000 creatives, activists, policy-makers and 'passionate humans' working collaboratively to drive action and awareness on the climate emergency.

When it comes to promoting change, Lucy believes that:

> Organisations have to look at their very reason for being. It has to be more than a campaign or a one-off action, or even just one aspect of their business. I want to know, what is the organisation willing to do at a structural level to prioritise the planet and its people?
>
> Are they committing to frameworks like the B-Corp certification? Are they willing to make nature a shareholder in the business? Are they willing to divest from using fossil fuels across their supply chain?
>
> Another key aspect to consider is how is that organisation behaving? The very system in which we are currently living, and I would even go so far as to say are indoctrinated into, is based on competition. That makes it incredibly hard for us as individuals, but even more so for organisations, to actually work collaboratively. But these issues demand it. Organisations are not faceless entities, but rather driven by human beings. We all have a responsibility to engage people emotionally in the work that they create.
>
> When shareholders and business leaders start to feel responsible for the outputs of their work, their organisation and their brand then the conversation will change. This requires a cultural shift but that is already starting to happen.
>
> We see it a lot with younger people who want their work to be aligned to their values. They feel a responsibility and a connection to the outputs of their organisation whether they work in fashion, avia-tion, food production or any other sector. People no longer have that kind of cognitive disconnect between their values and just turning up for work believing that nothing else is within their realm of influence.
>
> People are waking up to the reality that business leaders and decision-makers, particularly shareholders, have the power to create real change by committing to it from the inside out.

When it comes to brands and organisations being braver about making those sorts of commitments, especially in regard to climate change, Lucy believes that 'greenwashing' occurs when organisations are not fundamentally taking action.

> I think storytelling emerges from decisions that organisations are making to drive change and that actually committing to working in the space, like reducing carbon emissions or considering the life cycle of a product, enables brands and leaders to be braver. The bravery doesn't come out of nowhere. It comes from the evidence and proof gathered by stepping into the arena.

Organisations need to be afraid of what happens if they don't act because they are going to lose their social licence to operate. If they do not take radical action then not only will they lose their social licence to operate from consumers, but they will also become irrelevant in a world that needs to address issues such as food and water scarcity, and increased migration issues.

We have no choice but to reimagine the role that businesses will play in our future, and this is quite a daunting thought. Even the fruit we buy at the supermarket is still covered in plastic that we put in a bin. How are we still living in a system that is so polluting and so unsustainable?

Meanwhile, as Lucy speaks, her home country of New Zealand is flooding. She says: 'We are living in an apocalyptic emergency. We have to be brave enough to accept a radical reimagining of the way we live in a society and the actions that are now demanded of each and every one of us'.

The challenge of activists maintaining momentum is one that Lucy is all too aware of.

I honestly cannot believe that I have done this for almost five years. I don't know how I have maintained momentum. I haven't had enough funding, and I have maintained the momentum to keep fighting the good fight whilst becoming a mother and employing people all around the world.

On the other hand, I'd say that I maintain momentum because I have a lot of fun with the people that I connect with. It is also a space of possibility and innovation. Of joy and ruthless honesty. That is really exciting. I also get to connect with people in a way that I wasn't able to in a more corporate setting. That is the momentum I am able to bring when I work with corporation, and they appreciate the level of honesty that I bring to the room.

But the stark reality is that activists also need to maintain momentum with funding. There needs to be more recognition of that.

One of the difficulties I have found being visible as a change agent is that you are invited to so many platforms and places that want to have an activist in the room but how do I fund my time?

My answer is that there should be a reframing of this type of engagement as business insight and strategy. That would mean that the rates that organisations are willing to spend on having that voice in the room would be comparable with that available when you work in a polluting industry.

People should recognise that when you're working in the service of life and nature that requires reward. However, because our economy is so based on rewarding extractive behaviour, the 'profit' margin for activists just isn't there. The 'value to society' that we have put out there is deemed as being less valuable which it's not. So, how do we rethink those systems?

I saw something pop up in my feed the other day, which was asking whether putting a price on the value of a whale means that we take ocean conservation more seriously. That is such a post capitalist, insane, notion, and yet like the answer is quite possibly 'yes'. That maybe by putting a price on the value of a whale, we as human beings will preserve whales.

If we cannot value the right things in society, we will end up in the wrong place. The lower value assigned to activism remains a concern.

When it comes to the relationship between activists and businesses, Lucy believes that there are valuable lessons to be learned.

Activism, by its very nature, is very responsive to energy and ideas. Opportunities arise from conversations or statements made by organisations that activists then have a creative response to. There is a willingness to act. We have so little budget and the issues we are fighting for are so important that we have to act now. The attitude is like anything is better than nothing. That we don't have a lot which means we can't always be perfect about this.

I know that that happens with Creatives for Climate. We are superfast but we are experimental. We lean into others. We are radically honest and transparent in how we bring people along. Even our story resonates in a way that people haven't felt in a long time.

When people engage with Creatives for Climate, they are connecting with an entity that is full of engaged people trying to make things happen. That, in turn, helps to bring the public along on the journey. From a communications perspective, that is quite a big lesson, that you have to explain to organisations and brands.

Activists need to learn how to be better businesspeople, which is something I hate to say. But as someone running a frontline organisation, unless I can learn how to navigate big funding structures and come up with sustainable business models then I can't do the work I want to do.

But businesses too need to become genuine activists. They really need to emotionally engage with these issues and then challenge the way that they do things to make change happen.

There is a lot of sacrifice in activism. There is a lot of working in communities and working within larger movements that doesn't really allow for the kind of heroic narrative that we like to see in business.

That kind of humility in working towards greater causes is a thing that businesses and brands can learn from activists.

When it comes to activists and businesses working together, Lucy believes that both sides have a lot to consider.

I think it's tricky when there are more brands and businesses stepping into the space that traditional funding and philanthropy would have taken in the past. A lot of brands want to use changemakers or campaigns or offset some of their negative impacts by funding positive impact.

Brands need to look at the example of institutional organisations such as traditional grant making NGOs, ones that have had a longer legacy and history, to learn how they should engage with grantees. How they should honour the relationships with them. How to empower them and recognise that there is a power imbalance between funder and grantee.

That also means recognising that funding positive impact is actually about the positive impact, not about how many clicks you get on an organisation's newsletter or other such transactional measurements.

That is what we've experienced when dealing with some brands that want to support what we do. There is a huge difference between those funders that know what they are doing and are actually working in the interest of the cause, and those that are stepping into this space for their own interests. Grantees, like myself, know and feel the difference. Whilst there is a power imbalance, we are not so powerless anymore. Funders can start to develop bad reputations.

Whilst we need brands and businesses to step into funding positive impact, they need to do so in a way that isn't transactional. They need to honour the work of the NGOs and larger grant making entities that have come before them. They need to learn the lessons.

That is how brands can better work with activists. Number one is funding them. What we really need is funding for the work that we are well positioned to do.

Context

For Tessa Wernink, a business activist, coach and social entrepreneur, the context for activism has changed:

People born in 2000 (Generation Z), are entering the workforce. Much of this century has revolved around the climate crisis and these young professionals (and many Millennials) expect businesses to take action and take responsibility for their role in perpetuating social inequality and being responsible for environmental degradation.

While companies have become used to reacting to pressure from the outside to change their practices, internal pressure and how to deal with employee activists who are targeting their own organisation's (lack of) social and environmental performance is uncharted territory.

In the last century, employee activism in Europe fought for social justice, and through their hard fight, unionisation, works councils, whistleblowing hotlines were formed as structural parts of the business.

Today, young workers would like these instruments to become used proactively to highlight more issues, including underperformance on climate goals and greenwashing, or raise alarm on companies not living up to their values. Until then, young professionals have started informally organising around these issues at work. In employee resources groups and more.

But companies and management weren't educated in how businesses are expected to take a political stand. Their neoliberal MBAs taught them that the business of business was business. Taking a political stance as a company was rare. Dangerous. All that has since changed.

Companies are expected to have purpose, operate according to their values, take necessary action in their own supply chains, and speak up on political matters. And not just externally, but to have done the work internally. And if they haven't or have no intention to, they can now expect their (young) workforce to speak up, leave (climate quitting and conscious quitting), or new talent to not even consider them as a place to work.[21]

If you think companies can tap into dated playbooks that have helped them delay and lobby and deal with outside pressure, then you haven't been paying attention. While the media, civil society, NGO and citizen pressure is still strong, it's the employee who is disrupting the status quo in business. Internal pressure is growing, taking their political stance on wider social and environmental issues into workplaces, challenging hierarchies of power and demanding that companies become more ambitious in their goals. And companies can no longer superficially engage with these issues.

We discussed the best techniques for companies to listen to activists.

Activism is about dreams, values, and what people care about or want to protect. But that's not what everyone thinks when you say the word activist. Activism is a loaded term. And often senior leaders feel provoked, want to avoid conflict and perceive it as negative. And so a great first step is to listen to activists. And to do so, you need to understand your relationship with the term activism. What assumptions do you have and how does that influence your ability to listen?

Professor Megan Reitz has some great research in this area. She says that leaders sometimes live in optimism bubbles, that businesses sit on the fence when it comes to action and, most interestingly, she identifies a spectrum of responses from organisations to activism. It ranges from non-existent and suppression to facadism and defensive engagement to finally dialogic engagement and even stimulating activism.

The point is that as a senior leader, you are responsible for creating a space and a culture in which voices can speak up about issues that might not seem immediately relevant to day-to-day business. Because these issues are extremely relevant to corporate culture and the sense that your job is a meaningful contribution to achieving your company's mission.

While companies make space for whistle-blowers to call hotlines and anonymously raise flags on fraud, unethical behaviour and worse, the younger generation of employees think a business should accommodate for places where people can raise flags on not living up to your values, not doing enough to tackle climate change or hiring diverse people and accommodating inclusive environments. If you leave it to a whistle-blower, it's too late.

So, for managers to avoid negative conflict, they would be wise to focus on psychological safety. A first step is translating values into behaviours and habits. A second is calling out bullshit (i.e. when people keep telling the same jokes and nothing changes). It's really important that there are spaces in which external social and environmental issues and movements are brought into the business. And the best strategy is to empower employees to be a part of the solution.

There are many terms that have been coined that reframe what an activist does without the negative association. Think of the people in your business as changemaker, innovator, intrapreneur. And that the conflict arises when changemakers conflict with 'status-quo defenders'. Rarely is either of them fully right, but the conflict isn't about the people, it's about what needs to be addressed. It's time that activism got rid of the bad reputation, which is why we say that 'activism is love made visible'.

When it comes to how organisations should react when hearing negative comments from activists, Tessa believes that:

One of the most important skills anyone in this day of polarisation should learn is listening. Listening, not just hearing and then talking back. We work with young activists who are often disappointed, fed up, disillusioned, ready to quit. These feelings don't make for very inspirational listening, but it's too easy to put the negativity on the speaker.

In our trainings, we coach young employees to get in touch with their values, with what drives them, and embrace the things they care about. It's the first step to positive activism. To speaking up for what you want to change. And that is the work these employees are doing to be heard.

And likewise, senior leaders need to go the extra mile too. Can you listen with empathy? Can you hear what values they are speaking up for? Can you relate to their disappointment? If so, it's the starting point for courageous conversations.

The other thing to remember is that content is complex, and so we need to step into inquiry. 'Answers have short shelf lives, but a good question goes a long way'. We need to include the young generation's ideas and ambition into the solution to navigate the wicked problems many companies are facing.

In the words of Paul Polman – former CEO of Unilever and author of *Net Positive*, 'employees want to be part of the mission to improve their company's positive impact on the wider world. Their offer of collaboration is a tremendous opportunity for the CEOs who are ready to act. Trust me, if someone is ready to quite their job because of their values and because they believe business can profit while serving people and planet, that's someone you probably don't want to lose'.

I wondered if 'fighting back' against activists was ever a good reaction?

The answer is in the question, everyone knows that long term it's not a good reaction, but companies might think that silencing voices or threatening them is an effective way to get rid of a problem. When activists are alone and haven't managed to organise, by building coalitions or connecting to wider movements, it's possible to 'kill' the messenger or disruptive voice.

And so, we focus on how activists can organise around topics. As an employee activist you need to be aware that a company is not a democracy. And that if you put yourself in a vulnerable position, that your message dies with your 'removal'. You need to move from individual to collective action. And when you organise, and your coalition grows or you connect to wider movements, companies will have a harder time 'fighting back'.

We spend a lot of time working with our participants on allyship in all areas of the business. On analysing risks and knowing your rights. Discussing privilege and inequality and building solidarity groups. On not having leader-dependent movements, but all having a role to play. These are all tactics that come straight from activism everywhere and have helped suppressed voices throughout centuries to keep the fire burning.

In other words, you can fight back, and while it might temporarily cancel out the noise and 'kill the messenger', the message will return and probably bite the company in the ass. So, if you really want to 'make it go away', the best approach is engagement. It's dialogue.

Tessa and I explored what businesses and activists can learn from each other.

This can be answered on an individual level – how can employee activists use an activist mindset and strategies to be more effective in creating change. We developed a course with this in mind which culminated in the below learning journey as a way to illustrate some of the strategies.

Business changemakers can think like activists, putting the cause over personal gain, using conflict in a positive way, learning the skills of non-violence and listening.

How to grow your movement by connecting with colleagues over values, not function. Telling your story and demands in clear terms and mixing emotions with factual reasons.

Becoming strategic, connecting with the industry and always trying to formalise any achievements.

The way people move to action varies. Some people prefer what is termed tempered radicalism, small steps over time. Others prefer direct action, resistance and asking 'for forgiveness, not permission'. What is clear is that it's different for everyone and it differs per context how radical you can be. James Ozden talks about non-violent radical tactics being likely to increase support for more moderate groups in ways that increase a movement's overall chances of achieving their aims.[22]

The question can be answered on an organisational level too. How can businesses use an activist stance to forward their purpose? Because the idea of purpose is in many ways similar to having a cause. In that line of thinking, everything a business does should be in service of fulfilling its cause.

A great example is Patagonia of course, whose business operates to 'save our home planet'. While you could say that their core products do no such thing, they take precious materials from the earth and leave waste, the company has taken a more systemic look at what their company needs to do to fulfil this mission. That means looking beyond making their core product sustainable, for example by taking a political stand on issues around the destruction of national environments. Giving a percentage to activist causes, supporting documentaries that research problems and using advertising to change behaviour in positive ways that reduce consumption and nudge people to repair clothing. They recently established the Holdfast collective, which puts ownership of Patagonia with the planet, making sure the business structure stewards the company in achieving its mission.

Patagonia an activist company and has become a bastion of moral leadership in an age where employees are quietly and consciously quitting jobs that have no meaningful contribution to future generations. What we can learn is that your business is in business to serve its purpose. And that you need to trust your employees (not just your shareholders), to contribute to achieving that. That your senior leadership should be role-modelling what that looks like.

Lastly, what can activists learn from business? Perhaps here it's good to quote *The Entangled Activist* by Antra Lawson, who argues that activists can get entangled in the problems they seek to solve. This resonates with me as a social entrepreneur. I saw a lot of social entrepreneurs burning out because they couldn't separate their business from their personal cause. And in the fight forgot about self-care. Lawson points to another problem; she says that activism needs to be more than 'righteous reactivity', and perhaps this is where businesses environments can help. We need to include facts, trial and error and embrace that the problems we need to solve are complex. Nurture inclusive cultures and examine our shadows and assumptions.

I asked Tessa what role social entrepreneurs can play in this.

Social entrepreneurship in its most basic definition is using a business model to address and fix social and environmental issues. That means that impact and profit go hand-in-hand and that every decision made takes those two factors into account.

This has been an extremely important development in a world in which according to Milton Freedman the business of business is business – and not social or environmental responsibility. In that way, social entrepreneurship is an immensely important pioneer in leading the way to a new kind of business responsibility.

Moreover, social enterprises have a strong campaigning element – such as with Fairphone – the company I co-founded. Our aim was to raise awareness around social and environmental issues in the electronics supply chain and the first few phones were actually sold with the slogan, 'buy a phone, join a movement'. And this goes for many social enterprises. Sometimes due to lack of funding, but mostly the story was the marketing campaign. It sold the product through the story.

But besides campaigning, social enterprises use other strategies from activism, by disrupting industries that were never about values with value-based marketing, collaborating with the entire ecosystems to achieve their cause (not seeing them as competitors, but as collaborators on a mission-level), and raising the issue over the person.

That said, social entrepreneurship is still relatively small. B-Corps is another movement that is increasing in membership and becoming an example for how business can be a force for good – but it's not close to accelerating the change we need to see. For that to happen, we need people inside companies to become social intrapreneurs and activists and change their organisations inside-out and bottom-up.

The politics

Whilst being active does not have to mean being political, that does not mean that politicians will not feel the urge to get involved. A backlash can come from any stakeholder group with each inflicting their own type of damage. But dealing with politicians brings with it reputational and organisational challenges. Politicians have the power to make new laws and regulations and impose taxes. They can impact on the operations of any organisation.

Activist companies can find themselves in conflict with a range of audiences, but politicians are one of the most challenging to deal with.

The most high-profile example is the conflict taking place between Disney and Florida Governor, and former Presidential hopeful, Ron DeSantis. He has led a campaign again Disney following the company's decision to oppose the 'Don't Say Gay' law being proposed in the state. The bill, now passed, Parental Rights in Education (HB 1557), 'prohibits classroom discussion about sexual orientation or gender identity in certain grade levels'[23] amongst its other messages.[24]

Disney suspended its political donations to the state and began supporting organisations that were against the law. DeSantis removed a special planning status that the company enjoyed. Disney decided not to proceed with a new office complex and called the governor 'anti-business'.

DeSantis did not appear too upset to pick a fight with Disney, despite them being an important employer in the state. In a fundraising email, he said:

> Disney and other woke corporations won't get away with peddling their unchecked pressure campaigns any longer. If we want to keep the Democrat machine and their corporate lapdogs accountable, we have to stand together now.[25]

But politicians also like to weigh into such controversies when then know there is already an element of customer / voter support. In the case of the beer brand Bud Light, its work with transgender activist Dylan Mulvaney, to promote its product on Instagram, led to calls for a boycott. Its sales fell and profits dropped as the boycott grew.[26] The boycott secured high-profile supporters including musicians and, again Ron DeSantis. The initial response from the company was criticised for saying very little and Mulvaney complained about the lack of support she received. Executives lost their jobs, and the brand embraced a different approach to marketing.

In such circumstances, organisations can essentially choose to stand up and fight, or cave in. Bud Light chose to cave in; Disney carried on fighting. A company will have to decide what is best for them, but these are the types of scenarios that need to be considered before the initial action.

The relationship between politics and business can be a complicated one. Political parties and politicians often need the financial support of business and often welcome the endorsement of their leaders.

But the reality is that politicians can be activists as well. They are happy to use the same techniques as activist groups.

Scott Goodstein, founder of Catalyst Campaign which turns stories into action, was the external online director for Barack Obama's 2008 presidential campaign and was a lead digital strategist on Bernie Sanders's 2016 campaign. Scott and I discussed what activists should think about when seeking to influence businesses or governments:

Activists should always think about how their stance benefits the larger good. How does their group or organisation benefit not just their cause… but the greater good? Consider whether your issue brings in more revenue, improves the quality of life of a community, makes an area of the community safer, etc. For example, the SaveOurStages campaign in the United States during the pandemic was based on the independent venues being the first to close during the pandemic and the last to open. Most of the venues rented space in their neighbourhood. If this lobbying effort was just based on a private business renter of property wanting help, they would have been lumped in with every other small business and fought for a Small Business Association Covid-relief loan. However, these independent venues were able to pull together and build their own piece of legislation based on the cultural, community, and economic impact that each of these clubs has on their neighbourhood and how they are the business driver as well as the artistic centre for each Congressional District in America – both Democrat and Republican. Every community has a small independent stage that needed additional help to survive the pandemic. These club owners quickly created the National Association of Independent Venues, pulled their resources to tell their story, and passed the $16 billion dollar Save Our Stages Act through the House and Senate, and signed by the President of the United States.

When it comes to tactics that work well, economic studies, environmental studies, authentic stories, and people with personal connections can annunciate the desired change. You need both the math and the emotion to make a good campaign.

I asked Scott what had been the most significant changes in activist campaigns that he had seen? He pointed to three main changes.

First, the ability to record and quickly distribute video online, meaning City Hall and congressional meetings are no longer secretive.

Second, social media and hashtags. The ability for ordinary citizens to follow an issue online and collectively work on legislation together in real time. Whether this is following City Hall, county council, congress, school board meetings or even corporate shareholder meetings. Folks can follow the issue quickly, discuss it using the hashtag, distribute talking points, videos, calls to action, etc. Mobilisation no longer needs to wait for an organisation to have large discussions on which tactic they are going to use. Citizens can decide and mobilise for themselves, and create their own talking points, memes, shareable graphics, and rapid response actions.

Third, online mobilisation to quickly text your supporters and ask them to immediately contact their legislature. They can now text the legislator's phone number to a smartphone so that a supporter can just click on the number and call that legislator and let them know why the issue is important to them.

Considering how businesses or governments can respond effectively when facing an activist campaign, Scott suggested:

1   Listen!
2   Show that you are listening.
3   Engage the audience in a constructive way. Energy on issues is not always bad for governments, even when negative. Smart governments recognize that these are citizens, too, and they deserve to have their voice heard. Even if there is a disagreement, not hearing citizens speak or trying to silence the opposition's speech is usually ten times worse than just providing folks a real opportunity to have an honest discussion on the issue.

How did Scott believe that businesses best avoid an attack in the first place?

Test the change and ask for feedback – similar to how smart governments work. Allow citizens and the general public to engage with the change and discuss it. Learn why the change is happening and what they like and don't like about it. Listen and be flexible. You may end up rolling out a slightly different and even better product that has been adapted from hearing some feedback and engaging with those who will be using the product in the future!

Reflections

The sometimes fraught relationship between employees and business owners is nothing new, but as the example of Apple highlights there remain lessons for all. For businesses, it shows that they are not all powerful. Employees, even within large, successful companies where the value of a brand dominates, retain power. They know and understand this so understand the basis of the power they can wield. As the Apple example shows, heavy-handed managerial control can backfire. A management team can be focused on what they believe an organisation stands for but if the workforce does not agree then there can be a well-organised and effective backlash. Just as businesses need to listen to external communities, they must also listen to internal communities.

The Apple Together movement shows how employees, even at a high-profile tech giant, can band together to challenge corporate policies and demand change. By recognising the power of sharing stories and experiences through the #AppleToo campaign, these workers were able to publicly expose a gap between Apple's stated values and their actual treatment of employees. As with any other aspect of reputation, a gap is a risk and a danger.

Apple Together is a good example for other activists to learn from, as they are already doing. Holding an employer to account by using its own principles, missions or beliefs provides leverage. For Apple Together, their tactics of solidarity, collective action, and using social media to elevate individual stories proved highly effective at building public awareness and pressure on the company.

That is not to suggest that there are not significant challenges involved in employee activism. For some businesses it is viewed as a total negative rather than a potential source of strength and improvement. The focus for some may simply be on the immediate 'bottom line' whilst failing to appreciate that employees can help to avoid unnecessary costs and contribute to financial improvements. Addressing grievances is simply about adding costs. If businesses try to side-line or downplay internal dissent then it makes the task of activists more challenging but can, perversely, provide motivation and galvanise support.

With changing expectations, often values-based, of younger generations about work and the role of business, simply having a strong external brand will not be enough. Employees will continue to try to hold employers to account and this may even increase if leadership teams are not sufficiently responsive. Meaningful change can be delivered but only if businesses listen and internal activists utilise that opportunity.

Notes

1 Josh Graff, Managing Director, EMEA & LATAM & VP Global Enterprise, LinkedIn, 'Why strong company values are essential for attracting the next generation of professionals', World Economic Forum, 19 April 2023, www.weforum.org/agenda/2023/04/why-company-values-deal-breaker-next-generation-professionals/
2 Apple Together, https://twitter.com/AppleLaborers
3 Apple Together, https://appletogether.org
4 Jennifer Bisset, 'Marvel's VFX artists are suffering – and starting to speak out', CNET, 5 August 2022, www.cnet.com/culture/entertainment/marvels-vfx-artists-are-suffering-now-theyre-speaking-out/
5 Alphabet Workers Union, https://alphabetworkersunion.org/principles/mission-statement/
6 Herbert Smith Freehills, 'Future of work: Adapting to the democratised workplace', 2019, www.herbertsmithfreehills.com/latest-thinking/the-new-world-of-work-report-warns-of-an-unprecedented-rise-in-workplace-activism-v2

7 Megan Reitz and John Higgins, 'Leading in an age of employee activism', *MIT Sloan Management Review*, 19 January 2022, https://shop.sloanreview.mit.edu/store/leading-in-an-age-of-employee-activism

8 Dare To Lead with Brené Brown, 'Brené with Megan Reitz and John Higgins on leading in an age of employee activism', 28 February 2022, Spotify

9 Megan Reitz, 'Leading in an age of employee activism: The do's and don'ts', TEDxTalks, 16 June 2022, www.youtube.com/watch?v=zIz7eVfLs94

10 Megan Reitz, 'Leading in an age of employee activism: The do's and don'ts', TEDxTalks, 16 June 2022, www.youtube.com/watch?v=zIz7eVfLs94

11 B Corp, 'About B Corp certification', www.bcorporation.net/en-us/certification/

12 Masters of Scale: Rapid Response, 'Waging a $1.4 trillion food fight', 14 July 2022, https://mastersofscale.com/waging-a-1-4-trillion-food-fight-peter-mcguinness/

13 Masters of Scale: Rapid Response, 'Turning tears into action', 21 July 2022, https://mastersofscale.com/turning-tears-into-action/

14 Masters of Scale: Rapid Response, 'Turning tears into action', 21 July 2022, https://mastersofscale.com/turning-tears-into-action/

15 Masters of Scale, '5 ways to build your tolerance for risk', 4 October 2022, https://mastersofscale.com/5-ways-to-build-your-tolerance-for-risk/

16 The Marketing Journal, 'The case for brand activism: A discussion with Philip Kotler and Christian Sarkar', 15 November 2018, www.marketingjournal.org/the-case-for-brand-activism-a-discussion-with-philip-kotler-and-christian-sarkar/

17 Elizabeth Wiredu, 'Amazon apologises after UK Black History Month campaign backlash', *PR Week*, 25 October 2022, www.prweek.com/article/1802922/amazon-apologises-uk-black-history-month-campaign-backlash

18 Foundation for Public Affairs, 'Lobbying for good', 26 October 2021, https://pac.org/wp-content/uploads/Lobbying-for-Good.pdf; and Public Affairs Council, 'Taking a stand: How corporations engage on social issues', 26 October 2021, https://pac.org/wp-content/uploads/Taking-a-Stand.pdf

19 Prof Ana Adi, 'Corporate activism: Research, case studies and solutions for communicators to address a rising trend', Quadriga University of Applied Sciences, 2019, www.quadriga-hochschule.com/app/uploads/2021/03/QHS_Quadriga-Reader_Corporate-Activism_Adi.pdf

20 Sarah Murray, 'When should business take a stand', *Financial Times*, 9 March 2022, www.ft.com/content/5ceffa36-899a-4457-919f-b70902162f64

21 Paul Polman, '2023 net positive employee barometer: From quiet quitting to conscious quitting', February 2023, www.paulpolman.com/wp-content/uploads/2023/02/MC_Paul-Polman_Net-Positive-Employee-Barometer_Final_web.pdf

22 For more of James Özden's work see his Substack, 'Understanding social change', https://jamesozden.substack.com

23 Florida Senate, CS/CS/HB 1557: Parental Rights in Education

24 For more information on the measures see National Education Association, 'What you need to know about Florida's 'Don't Say Gay' and 'Don't Say They' laws, book bans, and other curricula restrictions', 2023, www.nea.org/sites/default/files/2023-06/30424-know-your-rights_web_v4.pdf

25 Ian Millhiser, 'Ron DeSantis's attack on Disney obviously violates the First Amendment', *Vox*, 23 April 2022, www.vox.com/23036427/ron-desantis-disney-first-amendment-constitution-supreme-court

26 Amanda Holpuch, 'Behind the backlash against Bud Light', *The New York Times*, 21 November 2023, www.nytimes.com/article/bud-light-boycott.html

Chapter 4

The legal approach
Shareholder activism and beyond

The legal route

Campaigners know and understand that the law can help them. It can motivate supporters, for instance, by helping them to crowdfund for a particular approach. It is also a good way of ensuring that those potentially on the receiving end of a legal challenge follow the right processes and procedures throughout. It is a way that activists can hold organisations to account and ensures adherence to the correct procedure.

A legal challenge can, often usefully, increase the profile of the issue with a range of wider stakeholder audiences. A legal approach never stands alone; it is part of an overall strategy. That could include media and stakeholder engagement. The actual legal avenue is only one aspect of the campaign. It could be a means to facilitate and develop other aspects of the campaign. Whilst it would obviously be better for the activists if the legal approach is successful, in some ways it does not need to be. This is an important realisation for all sides.

Laws and court decisions can also serve as a catalyst for activism, as they may inspire people to organise and advocate for change in response to perceived injustices. In some instances, activists may use civil disobedience and other forms of direct action to draw attention to issues and pressure lawmakers to take action. These actions may lead to arrests, and activists may use their trials as a platform to bring attention to their cause. They may almost dare lawmakers to take action which they know will be publicly unpopular so will exert pressure.

Overall, activism and law are increasingly intertwined, with the law providing a framework for activism, and activism using the legal system to help secure change.

An article by FTI illustrates this with reference to the rise of environmental litigation against large businesses. It suggests that challenge could arise in three main areas:

- shareholder litigation for financial misstatement on ESG disclosure

DOI: 10.4324/9781003371908-5

- consumer protection and competition regulators investigating misleading product claims
- a rise in third-party litigation funding for group actions on environmental harm.[1]

The article states, based on supporting research, that 'One-in-five of business leaders believe that the majority of their company's communications on the environment is simply greenwashing'. Even that statement will give activists grounds for optimism when considering the prospects of a successful legal challenge, and should, in turn, focus the minds of business leaders.

The same, it could be suggested, is true for governments as well. The UK government has been forced to the courts on many occasions, not least on its Net Zero commitments. Just as business leaders can have their minds focused by a legal challenge, so can governments.

According to *The Guardian*, 2023 was going to be a watershed year for climate litigation – and so it seemed to be.[2]

US activist courts

The position in the US is influenced by the existence of its written constitution. That has led to the suggestion that there are 'activist courts'. It is a term used to suggest that some courts interpret and apply laws in a way that favours particular political or ideological agendas. For instance, the way in which the Supreme Court interprets the Constitution and laws can be more liberal or conservative than previous court decisions. The membership of the Supreme Court is said to be important in such cases which makes appointing members by the President, with ratification by Congress, so important. One of the undoubted achievements of the Trump presidency was the appointments he made to the Supreme Court, and the blocking by the Senate beforehand of President Obama's nominee, Merrick Garland.

In the past it was suggested that the Supreme Court had liberalised the country through cases such *Roe v Wade* and *Brown v Board of Education*. There is a massive body of literature and discussion about this issue, which I cannot claim to have captured in any meaningful way, but there is little doubt that Donald Trump made appointments to the Supreme Court a key part of his election platform as he understood the impact that could be made.

One of the outcomes of Trump's three appointments was arguably the Court's decision to rule there is no constitutional right to abortion in the United States, meaning that each state has the individual choice about whether to allow it or not.[3] This apparently settled issue, right back to *Roe v Wade*, blew up again. It was a polarising issue in any case but the change in the law had the effect of galvanising people. The decisions made by the Court invigorated the campaign for women's reproductive rights.

There followed a huge outcry from liberal politicians, celebrities and campaigners alike. Despite the Supreme Court ruling, anti-abortion activists continue the fight in individual states, and it should be noted that according to polling, there is majority support for abortion rights in the country.[4]

The mid-term elections in the November following the decision saw Democrats do better than expected and, in every state where an abortion-related measure was on the ballot, voters chose either to enshrine protections or reject new limits.

It is clear that this Supreme Court decision had direct political consequences because of campaigning activity.

Rise of crowdfunding

Crowdfunding is often considered in relation to gaining finance for start-ups, but it is now also part of the activist playbook. Many organisations use crowdfunding as a way of raising finance for activist measures, especially to launch legal challenges.

One such platform is CrowdJustice, which collects pledges of funding. As it states, 'people have raised amounts from as little £300 for initial advice, to more than £300,000 for more complex legal matters'.[5]

In essence, an individual can share a story about an issue they want to challenge and then try to secure backers for that campaign. What sites such as CrowdJustice also do is connect with lawyers so that the site user can raise the funds and the lawyer can accept them.

Just as crowdfunding democratises company ownership, such sites mean that everyone, at least in theory, can follow a legal option. For many this is liberating as the costs involved would otherwise be prohibitive. That means the legal option is no longer the preserve of corporates, large organisations or wealthy individuals.

By collecting together small contributions, individuals or smaller organisations can raise the funds to explore and possibly launch a legal action. It helps to motivate supporters and provides them with a clear indication that they are playing a meaningful role in the campaign.

Helen Fry is a Counsel at the Good Law Practice, an independent legal firm, part of the Good Law Project. The Project is a not-for-profit campaign organisation that uses the law for a better world.

I spoke to Helen about the role that the legal system can play in holding businesses and governments to account.

> Judicial review provides a means of challenging unlawful decisions by government, or other public bodies – it's a vital safeguard against the state acting beyond its powers, or outside the bounds of reason.
>
> At its broadest, judicial review can be used to challenge high-profile decisions or policies affecting the whole country. For example, in 2019

the Good Law Project and others brought a claim challenging the government's prorogation of Parliament; the Supreme Court ruled that the prorogation was nullified and reaffirmed an important constitutional limit on the power of the Executive.

Judicial review can also be used to challenge policies or practices impacting a particular group, often in the form of test cases brought by affected individuals. At its narrowest, it can be used to challenge a decision that affects only one person.

Private companies, of course, don't owe the same duties to the public as the government does, and they can't be subject to judicial review challenge unless they are performing a public function. They do, however, have to comply with the law, and they owe legal duties to stakeholders (for example their shareholders). NGOs are increasingly seeking to hold businesses to account for their harmful actions, filling the void left by inadequate government oversight. ClientEarth has recently brought a case against Shell, for example, which argues that the company's failure to move away from fossil fuels represents a risk not just to the planet, but to the viability of the business, and as such amounts to a breach of the trustees' duties to shareholders.

Often both government and business play a role in creating a problem, and resolving it requires a multi-faceted approach. Good Law Project's attempts to force action on sewage dumping in British waterways is a good example. They've intervened in a private law claim in which the owner of the Manchester Ship Canal is seeking to establish that United Utilities' dumping of sewage in the canal is unlawful; the decision will have broader implications for other waterways, and the object of the intervention is to ensure that those broader concerns are before the court. At the same time, Good Law Project is supporting a judicial review against the Department for Environment, Food and Rural Affairs, arguing that its plan to tackle sewage discharges by water companies (including United Utilities) doesn't go far or fast enough, and is therefore unlawful.

When it comes to activists using the law, Helen believes that there are many ways in which it can be used to advance their objectives.

Some organisations use the law at a grassroots level, helping individuals to enforce their rights. The charity Shelter, for example, has a long track record of advising individuals about – and empowering them to enforce – their housing rights, whether against public bodies or private landlords.

Another approach (and one that can grow from grassroots work) is strategic litigation, where organisations bring (or support) test cases to challenge a particular policy or practice. Such cases aim to achieve justice for the individual claimant/s and set a helpful precedent for others who are similarly affected, while at the same time building public awareness of the issue and pressure for change. This is the kind of work Good Law Project focuses on – either bringing claims itself or (depending on the circumstances) supporting directly impacted individuals to mount a challenge, often working closely with activists and specialist groups to build both the legal claim and the wider campaign. Judicial reviews have to be brought promptly, and in any event within three months of the decision under challenge, so time for this work can be tight.

As well as developing their own claims, some organisations seek to 'intervene' in cases that are likely to have a wider impact (whether or not they were intended as test cases). By intervening in third party litigation, an organisation can use its expertise to set out the potential ramifications of the outcome – which the parties themselves might not be focused on – for the court.

Rather than formally intervening, organisations can also look to provide witness statements (or expert reports) within third party litigation. In appropriate cases, this is a relatively light-touch way of making sure that their particular perspective and expertise are considered.

It's also possible to engage with a proposed law or policy before it comes into effect. Many activists and campaigning groups will respond to consultations about proposed changes to the law, for example, or lobby MPs and peers to make amendments to draft legislation as it passes through Parliament.

Costs though can, as highlighted, be a challenge when it comes to the use of the law so their management should be an important consideration for activists.

Parties to litigation face two potential sets of costs. First, the fees of their own lawyers (if they choose to instruct lawyers rather than representing themselves). And second, the defendant's costs, which they will usually be ordered to pay if they lose (an 'adverse costs' order).

Claimants will usually recover some, but not all, of their own costs if they win, but winning can of course never be guaranteed. For test cases raising important issues, it might be possible to find lawyers to act on a pro bono (free) basis, on reduced rates, or on a 'no win, low fee' basis (where lawyers agree to accept a lower fee if the case is not successful, and costs can't be recovered from the other side). Crowdfunding is also an important tool for lots of claimants who are pursuing issues of broader public interest.

The level of the defendant's costs are obviously outside of your control, and the prospect of a vast adverse costs order is enough to put off many litigants. But there are mechanisms designed to prevent concerns about costs from deterring meritorious claims.

Claimants bringing judicial reviews can ask the court to impose a cost capping order ('CCO'), which will limit their potential adverse costs exposure (as well as limiting the costs they'll be able to recover if they win). The courts can grant CCOs where the proceedings are in the public interest, and where the claimant would, without a CCO, reasonably withdraw the claim. The court will also take into account the financial resources of the parties, which means claimants will need to provide information about their financial position and any financial support they are receiving. However, CCOs cannot be granted unless and until permission to proceed is granted by the court, meaning pre-permission costs cannot be limited – such costs are not meant to be excessive, but it is a crucial factor to bear in mind.

There are also particularly robust protections, under the Aarhus Convention, for claimants bringing environmental challenges. Aarhus requires signatory states to ensure that claimants can access environmental justice in a way that's not prohibitively expensive. As a starting point, the court will cap costs in an Aarhus claim so that the claimant won't be ordered to pay more than £5,000 (if they're an individual) or £10,000 (if it's an organisation), and the defendant won't have to pay more than £35,000.

In any civil litigation, an awareness that the other side is incurring costs for which you could be liable can be a powerful motivation to settle, which is generally a good thing. But in public law challenges – where the claimant is often an individual or a campaigning group, and the defendant is often a central government department – that dynamic can be more one-sided, and the opportunities for compromise can be much more limited. Government departments have substantial legal teams at their disposal, with the potential to run up costs very quickly, and they know that they will generally be able to meet any adverse costs orders made against them.

Good Law Project has increasingly seen government run up extremely high costs in defending its judicial reviews, in particular those relating to the award of procurement contracts during the pandemic. In one of those cases, the Defendant (the Secretary of State for Health and Social Care) failed to provide an estimate of his legal costs for several months despite the Good Law Project's requests. When he finally did, he had already spent £600,000, and estimated that his total costs would reach £1.2m. And he argued that these weren't the kind of public interest proceedings where a CCO could be imposed – i.e. he wanted the Good Law Project to be on the hook for the full £1.2m if it lost. The Good Law Project – and presumably almost any other claimant – would have had to abandon the claim rather than carry an adverse costs risk of that size. In the event, the Court imposed a CCO of £300,000, meaning that the Good Law Project could continue the proceedings. But it is to be hoped that defendant costs of that level are not going to become the new norm, given the serious implications that could have for access to justice.

A challenge arises when deciding how best the legal approach should be supported by other forms of activity. As Helen explained to me:

> At its best, strategic litigation is one part of a jigsaw, combining with a broader campaign to raise awareness and push for change. The value of establishing a new precedent is minimal if other people who might benefit from it don't know about it, or if caseworkers/advisers in the relevant space aren't made aware of its implications. And a new precedent can always be overturned by Parliament if the government thinks they can do so without too much pushback.
>
> Running a campaign alongside a test case allows you to build public awareness of the issue and support for change. A successful campaign can shore up public support for a test case victory and make it less likely that government will reverse its effects. And a campaign around a case can have huge value in documenting an issue or injustice and pushing it up the agenda, even if the case doesn't succeed in court.
>
> A strong legal case alongside an effective campaign can also secure concessions, or even complete capitulation, before a claim's even been filed. The Good Law Project have in several cases intensified the spotlight on an issue through a threatened legal challenge, only for the defendant to back down in the face of mounting public pressure. For example, a proposed challenge to the government over free school meals during the pandemic, and a threatened claim against the Met Police over its initial refusal to investigate 'Partygate', were both swiftly followed by U-turns.

The use of the law, as with other form of activism, can learn and take inspiration from the types of activities employed in other countries. Helen agrees that lawyers can learn a lot from successful legal challenges in other countries. She warns though that:

> There's rarely a precise overlap, given that we are dealing with different laws and different legal systems. In the sewage dumping judicial review referred to earlier, for example, one of the grounds of challenge is that the government's discharge reduction plan breaches the Public Trust Doctrine, which says that the State holds coastal waters 'on trust' for the public and has a duty to protect them. That's a novel argument in England, but similar grounds have been successfully run in the USA, where the doctrine (inherited from English law) has become a central feature of environmental law in many States. That kind of cross-pollination of approaches and ideas can be fruitful, though legal cases (and campaigns) will always have to be developed in a local context.

Shareholder activism

Shareholder activism is nothing new, but it has become more important. It is another option for activists that utilises a legal route within the existing corporate legal framework.

This form of activism utilises the power of a shareholding, sometimes quite limited in number, and the voting rights it brings to change a company's policies or approach. The use of the voting rights brings with it a platform as well. The general fall in campaigning costs has helped shareholder activists as much as anyone else.

The activists can bring to the attention of a wider audience the financial performance, investments, behaviours, financial rewards for executives, long-term strategy etc., which all helps in their campaign.

There is no one approach when it comes to shareholder activism. Its rise in popularity as an option was driven by factors including the increasing availability of information about companies' financial performance, and changed governance practices, as well as changes in the legal and regulatory environment. Taken as a whole this made it easier for shareholders to organise and exert influence. It does also mean that opportunities vary between jurisdictions.

Early on, shareholder activism was often perceived as action led by a high-profile, slightly 'maverick', and often hugely successful, individual such as T. Boone Pickens.[6]

But shareholder activism has become more widespread and highly organised. Buying shares in a company brings with it rights, not least voting rights. The number of shares required can vary between companies; sometimes the numbers can be quite low. Activists buying into companies has changed the way in which company votes are viewed. No longer are they simple endorsements of a management's position but instead need to be considered and debated. This brings a more effective level of scrutiny and transparency. In turn, this brings more spotlight and media attention. The chances of success in opposing a management position may not always be high, although there are examples of defeat, but the fact that the position has to be explained and defended changes the mindset of leadership.

Shareholder activism has become a powerful tool for promoting corporate accountability and governance, and it is a popular and influential force in the business world.

According to Lazard's 'Annual review of shareholder activism 2023':

> 2023 activity reached a record high, topping the prior record set in 2018. Europe and APAC (Asia-Pacific) were the largest contributors to the spike in activity, with each experiencing record levels of new campaigns.[7]

The report found 252 new campaigns globally in 2023, representing a 7% increase year-on-year and the busiest year on record.

There can be a tendency to believe that shareholder activists simply seek to improve environmental performance, governance arrangements or challenge executive pay. There are though examples where activists want a better financial performance, more profits or higher dividends for shareholders. Shareholder activist campaigns can have various aims.

The evidence on the financial performance of a firm following activist action is mixed. Some claim that firms experience an immediate decline in profitability whilst reflecting that the effects in subsequent years are unclear.[8]

However, one literature review painted a more mixed picture before suggesting that 'firm performance can be enhanced if a firm's management works in collaboration with activist investors'.[9]

There are many examples of successful shareholder activism, across a range of sectors. ClientEarth pointed to:

- Three directors voted onto the board at Exxon.
- Chevron shareholders vote to reduce scope 3 emissions.
- Shareholders vote in favour of climate action plan for Spanish airport operator Aena.
- HSBC shareholder resolution about fossil fuel risk exposure.[10]

The Harvard Law School Forum on Corporate Governance is a useful resource on campaigns and includes statistics as well.[11]

Companies have often taken a quite combative approach when it comes to shareholder activists. Defeating them becomes the focus rather than engagement. They can seek to do this by building strong relationships with large institutional investors such as pension funds and mutual funds, making it more difficult for activists to gain control.

However, large-scale disputes held in public rarely help so instead companies have taken to:

- Developing a clear story about their strategy, performance, and future plans can help to build support among shareholders. This can make it more difficult for activists to gain traction for their approach.
- Being more transparent and opening themselves up to more regular engagement.

Arguably the most effective approach is to take pre-emptive action. This would typically include:

- building a strong and independent board of directors
- reviewing and strengthening corporate governance policies
- taking a robust approach to risk management and ESG matters.

That really means that the sheer threat of shareholder activism has a direct impact on the operation of an organisation. But maintaining such awareness should be an ongoing process. The danger of not doing so would be to fail to keep up with expectations of behaviour or to fall behind the actions and behaviour of competitors leaving them at a potential commercial disadvantage.

In reaction to shareholder activism, there have been examples of companies inviting an activist onto their board, for instance 'activist investor' Nelson Peltz joining the board of Unilever after his fund purchased a stake in the business. His activist, hands-on approach was welcomed.

> Sources said that Unilever's board had agreed to hand Peltz a board seat, despite owning a small stake in the company, after shareholders had privately encouraged bosses to welcome the activist. Investors flagged Peltz's long track record of reviving shareholder returns at his target companies and the expensive proxy battle with Procter & Gamble in 2017, which resulted in Peltz claiming a board seat and overseeing a turnaround of the company.[12]

But it could easily be that different parts of a business feel differently about the actions of activists. The board could see activists as a potentially valuable partner; the management could be suspicious of the activists' motives and how they question managements' approach; employees could have a range of views but may worry about the job implications of an activist campaign; and shareholders could be worried about the financial implications.

These differing views demonstrate the complexity of the relationship between activists and different parts of a business and highlight the importance of effective communication and collaboration between all parties involved.

Divestment

As well as shareholder activists challenging businesses on issues of behaviour, remuneration, etc., there are increasing numbers of examples of activists forcing change over investment strategies and of larger institutional investors withdrawing from certain sectors. Originally this was tobacco and then defence, but has now moved on to fossil fuels as well.

Investors themselves are likely to come under pressure if they are putting funds into businesses operating in controversial activities or are involved in controversial practices. Activities such as deforestation, human rights violations and other ESG issues may be considered as a reputational risk for investors. Again, expectations change over time so investment profiles could change as a result.

One of the most high-profile changes to investment came when the Church of England, as mentioned previously, confirmed that it was moving away from fossil fuels as the Church of Sweden had in 2014.

But the actions of the Church of England across other parts of its portfolio demonstrate that assumptions should never be made about what a shareholder activist looks like. There is no single type of activist organisation or individual, they come in a variety of forms. In the Church's case, for instance, they worked with others including the Swedish government pension fund (AP7), to commence legal action against Volkswagen after it refused to table its climate lobbying proposal. It claimed that it was 'beyond the competence of shareholders' but the Church disagreed.[13]

This also demonstrates that activists are prepared to mix and match their approaches.

I spoke to McKenzie Ursch at Follow This about the work of the organisation that 'unites small and big shareholders in oil to become a powerful voice that demands change'.[14] We began by discussing the key factors behind the formation of the campaign.

Mark van Baal, our founder, started Follow This in 2015. He was originally an engineer, but upon becoming aware of the climate crisis, felt a duty to do something about it. This led to a career in journalism, believing that if he could create enough public awareness about the situation and its consequences, the necessary changes would follow suit. However, after almost a decade of doing this work and not seeing any movement, he sought another route to make a change.

Seeing that oil majors are one of the leading contributors to climate change, he felt they were one of the key actors who needed to make a change. Yet, these companies seem not to listen to the public and manage to prohibit or otherwise evade the necessary policy intervention from governments. The one group they would listen to, to which they were beholden, were their shareholders.

After seeing the work of CIFF director Chris Hohn, and his capacity to affect the choices made by certain Dutch banks with only a small stake in the company, he wanted to transpose this model to the workings of oil companies. Accordingly, he worked to file our first resolution at Shell in 2015.

This required attaining enough shares to file the resolution. Under the UK companies act, in order to file a resolution, it is required to have either a 5% stake in the company, or to form a group of 100 shareholders with an average paid of capital of approximately 50,000 GBP. As the former figure would be in the millions if not billions of pounds, he elected to take the latter. Through diligent work and a charismatic personality, he established a strong rapport with a number of wealthy shareholders in the company who shared his chagrin with the company's lack of action on the climate crisis. Amassing a group of around 10 such individuals allowed him to meet the capital threshold in absolute terms. But he still needed to find around 90 other shareholders in the company. He brought forward the simple idea of individuals buying one share in the company who supported the company making a change. With a lot of networking and public speaking, he eventually hit the threshold of number of shareholders as well.

This allowed the filing of the first Follow This resolution at Shell. The resolution read 'Shareholders support the company to invest 100% of its profits in renewable energy'. While very well intentioned, it was out of touch with the needs of the investor community who were dis-inclined to support such a prescriptive request. However, the resolution still managed to garner around 2% of the votes at the company's AGM, which is sizable for such a resolution, especially considering that share-holders typically vote congruent to the management's recommendation, which in this case was against our resolution.

With this, the seeds of Follow This were planted. It demonstrated that such a grassroots movement was possible, that the individual investor could play a part in the climate crisis, that it was not com-pletely under the control of the large institutional investors.

In subsequent years, Follow This worked to refine its resolution, better understanding and accommodating the needs of investors; the resolution was drafted in a way which did not compromise on the cen-tral goal of Follow This's mission, that the company adopt a Paris Aligned strategy, but left complete discretion to the management for the implementation of that strategy.

We went on to discuss how the campaign has managed to maintain and build momentum:

After our first resolution, we began more substantial engagement with the company, as well as with its investors. Many investors see addres-sing the climate change not only as a moral imperative, but increasingly understand it to be a part of their fiduciary responsibility to their cli-ents. Should climate change come to pass, the effects on society, including the global economy, would be catastrophic. After many con-versations with investors, we better understood how to communicate that a vote in favour of our resolution is in their best interest; both as it is in the best interest of the company as well as in the best interest of their portfolio.

This required a lot of networking and cold calling. Investors varied in their willingness to engage with us. We worked to establish ourselves as less of an activist group and more as part of the investor community. All of the team at Follow This feels a moral compulsion to address climate change. However, this is not the key argument brought forth to investors. We approach it from an investor angle, aiming to become an honest broker of the truth. We are able to analyse company policy and inform investors about the contradictions and shortcomings of their climate strategies. Oil majors are adept at concealing and obfuscating the inconsistencies in their climate strategies and conveying themselves as responsible actors. However, their business models are entrenched in oil and gas; they have little imagination therebeyond.

- Value of dedicated volunteer network – every employee of Follow This started out as a volunteer.
- Being consistent in our ask and coming back to the companies and investors year on year with the same fair request: Paris-aligned emissions targets (who can argue with that?!).
- Providing consistent content in the media – which helps build public awareness and pressure for change surrounding investors' approach to stewardship and oil and gas companies' strategies. Our primary focus is to create clarity and transparency on what is and isn't being done and who is industry-leading and who is industry-lagging. We have cultivated important and longstanding relationships with a number of major press institutions and individual journalists who see us as an honest broker of the truth.
- Building strong relationships with influential investors in the Netherlands, leveraging those relationships to open doors for other contacts points and build our legitimacy/investor trust; working closely with investor alliances to call in other investors – essentially tapping into existing investor networks.

We explored what tactics have worked for the campaign with McKenzie highlighting two key ones:

Embracing the duality of Follow This and using it to our advantage. We are a climate NGO with clear environmental motivation and vision, but we also represent more than 9000 individual shareholders in oil and gas companies who have a legal stake in demanding action from these companies on climate; this allows us to relate and collaborate with both activists / other NGOs as well as businesses and investors.

And

Integrating organizational learning. The landscape changes over time and you need to pivot when necessary. A key aspect of this is building and co-designing tactics with others working in the space – such partnerships help in discerning promising steps forward and help to manage risks.

I asked McKenzie how they had found relations with the private sector:

> Each of the Follow This climate resolutions ends with the statement, 'we support you'. Our conviction is that we will not achieve the energy transition unless some of the largest fossil fuel companies make it with us, and the largest fossil fuel companies won't survive the transition unless they decide to be part of it. Thus, we see our role as a supportive one, in which we aim to give oil majors a shareholder mandate to transition for the good of their business and to the benefit of the world for generations to come.
>
> Our supportive attitude has not always been met with open arms by the industry. Oil and gas majors have repeatedly advised shareholders against our resolution and taken measures to side-step accountability for their emissions. In 2017, near the beginning of our campaign, Shell called our request for Paris-consistent emission reduction targets 'unreasonable'. As attitudes on emissions responsibility have changed, and more investors realize the financial risk posed by the heightening intensity of the climate crisis driven by the fossil fuel economy, Shell has developed this argument from 'unnecessary' in 2018–2021, to 'unrealistic' in 2022.
>
> In 2020, BP offered to draft a proposal together with us which would be presented to shareholders and backed by management the following year. In return, Follow This withdrew our resolution. Ultimately though, BP wouldn't go beyond a resolution that supported their existing climate targets, which included an increase in emissions in the next crucial decade. So, in 2021 we went on to file our resolution requesting the company set Paris-consistent targets which achieved double the support from investors than it had in 2019. Generally, the oil companies have been averse to our efforts to improve their targets, but more and more investors consistently prioritize climate commitments and recognize the risk that companies take by lagging on climate issues.
>
> Follow This cultivates close relationships with investors who hold shares in large oil and gas companies. Since we began filing resolutions in 2015, we have gradually built a coalition of the top ten Dutch investors in Shell who, for the first time, all voted in favour of the Follow This resolution in 2022. Over the course of the year, and particularly in the run up to the AGMs, we meet with as many investors as possible to discuss how to make company engagement impactful, how to escalate engagement tactics, and what purpose our resolution serves at each company. This year, we have even co-filed our resolutions with institutional investors representing 1.3 billion euros in AUM. We see our role with investors as an encouraging one, where we take on the risk of taking more stringent stances on company climate policy to pave a way for investors who may feel more nervous about possible implications

regarding their relationship with the company. This is not to say we don't call out poor stewardship from investors; we have a reputation for being an honest broker of the truth in the media regarding financial stewardship for the climate and the fiduciary duty of investors to demand attention to climate risk. But generally, we maintain positive relationships with most investors.

We discussed the biggest obstacles that Follow This has faced and how they have been overcome:

Building the movement outside of its origin country; it requires a deeper understanding of the contextual differences (how receptive people are, legislative requirements, prominent actors and potential partners).

One example of understanding and overcoming a legislative hurdle in a new jurisdiction occurred in the 2020–2021 season. This was the first year we aimed to file our climate resolutions in the US. However, the SEC had a robust and stringent legal framework by which companies could request permission from the SEC to exclude shareholder proposals. There were many different grounds on which this request for exclusion could be based; companies would often cite many of them, even if they contradicted each other (for example, claiming a proposal was both too prescriptive and too vague). In order to ensure our proposals made it to a vote, special care had to be paid to the drafting of our resolution. We refined our request word by word, ensuring that it would thread the needle through these often-imbricated exclusionary grounds. This required a careful analysis of past proposals and companies' attempts to have them excluded. We responded to companies' letters requesting exclusion, rebutting each of the arguments raised. In the end, the SEC decided in our favour in four out of four cases. Three out of four went on to receive a majority of shareholder's votes. The fourth was withdrawn after negotiation with the company which resulted in them satisfying our request. This endeavour further contributed to a revision of these overly capricious grounds of exclusion, seeing the SEC rewrite their standards of interpretation. They enhanced the rights of shareholders, allowing them to request more effective action from their investee companies for issues such as climate change.

Another obstacle was having our proposal properly filed and voted on in France. This entailed many different hurdles. The first of which was meeting the threshold required to file the resolution. Different jurisdictions have different procedural requirements which must be met in order to table a resolution; for example, the threshold of shares held in order to file. In France, proponents must hold 0.5% of all outstanding shares. In the case of a large company such as TotalEnergies, this meant finding investors who collectively owned approximately 1 billion euros worth of shares. This was no small feat; while multiple investors may be willing to vote in favour of our proposal, far fewer are willing to put their name on it and file it with the company. However, at the 11th hour, we managed to find a coalition of supportive investors with the necessary holdings to file. However, this was not the end of complications with this endeavour; despite meeting the procedural requirements necessary in order to file, the company unilaterally decided to reject our resolution and preclude it from coming to a vote. In their reasoning, they cited an almost century-old court case, the judgement of which is ambiguous and only loosely analogous to the issue at hand. The judgement of this case stated that issues of 'strategy' were to remain the purview of management. However, it provides no clarity or definition as to what strategy encompassed. There is certainly some justification that certain aspects of a business should be dealt with by management; the complexity and complications of the daily operations of a company require oversight which cannot be provided once per year at the company's annual meeting. However, an issue such as whether the company adopts a Paris-aligned framework to reduce its emissions is a high-level consideration which shareholders certainly have a right to voice their opinion on. In order to deal with this issue, we have been working with various French NGOs and legal professionals to lobby the French market regulator to make a statement about this, asserting that such proposals are appropriate for a shareholder vote. This will help not only our mission but help to protect the rights of shareholders more generally.

The newest hurdle is maintaining momentum among concerns of energy security following the outbreak of Russia's war in Ukraine and the resulting impact on global energy markets. This war once again exposed our dependence on oil and gas. While citizens faced towering energy bills, the oil and gas giants reported windfall profits. The energy crisis caused the fossil fuel industry to regain its self-confidence to continue with their unsustainable business model and managed to convince investors that the only solution to this crisis is investing more in oil and gas. This resulted in fewer investors voting in favour of our climate resolutions in May. This season, we face the challenge of convincing investors that both the climate crisis and the energy crisis must be dealt with by using current windfall profits to invest in renewables which will reduce our dependency on oil and gas fields impacted by geopolitical conflicts.

I wondered what McKenzie thought success would look like for their work:

One of the biggest achievements of Follow This to date is getting Scope 3 emissions on the agenda for oil and gas companies and their investors. Prior to our shareholder resolutions, no oil and gas major had set emission reduction targets which included accountability for their Scope

3 emissions – the emissions of their products. For companies selling fossil fuels as their business model, emissions of their products generally count for more than 90% of their total emissions portfolio. Only after investors have shown that they believe scope 3 emissions are the responsibility of the company by voting for Follow This resolutions have companies set targets to address them.

Additionally, our membership base has grown from 0 to nearly 10,000 members. We believe that Follow This provides people with a unique opportunity to participate in boardroom decisions and feel empowered to effect change at the biggest emitters in a way that is usually inaccessible to regular people. Follow This has presented the general public with information and means to get accountability from corporate emitters and demand another kind of energy system from those best-placed to effect change.

He cited particularly notable achievements in the last two years as being:

In 2021, we:

- Expanded our geographic focus. We navigated the American legislative landscape and were able to incorporate American oil and gas companies into focus. As a result, we successfully filed climate resolutions at seven oil and gas companies – three European (Shell, BP and Equinor) and four American (ConocoPhillips, Phillips66, Chevron and Occidental Petroleum – which was subsequently withdrawn after engagement).
- Filed 3 watershed climate resolutions at Chevron, ConocoPhillips and Phillips66, all of which received a majority vote (>50%). This breakthrough was facilitated by the SEC's – the enforcer of regulations on shareholder proposals and corporate governance in the US – change in attitude towards the exclusion of climate proposals in general and a corresponding expansion in terms of what shareholder proposals can request more generally. Had we not pushed the boundaries of what has conventionally been permitted by SEC regulations, we would not have seen this result. The SEC even uses the Follow This 2021 climate resolution at ConocoPhillips to illustrate that requests for climate targets are not micro-managerial. Our climate resolutions had ground-breaking impacts on re-shaping legislative practices in the US and have had a lasting impact on what can be achieved by others to get climate on companies' agendas moving forward.
- Successfully grew investor support for the Follow This climate resolution in Europe. At Shell, the Follow This resolution was pitted directly against a climate resolution submitted by management. Prior

to the AGM we worked to solicit investor votes – our engagement resulted in a twofold increase in votes for the Follow This resolution, and a <90% majority for Shell's proposal (management resolutions usually obtain about 95–99%). At BP and Equinor, votes in favour of the Follow This Climate Resolution doubled, representing 21% and 39% (of non-governmental shares) majority votes respectively.

In 2022, we:

- Testified in Congress as part of an ongoing investigation into Big Oil's complicity in misleading the public about climate change. At the hearing, we demonstrated that the climate pledges of ExxonMobil, Chevron, Shell and BP are not Paris-aligned, and illustrated these companies' reluctance to advance these targets. This was a huge step in the American public's acknowledgement of the contributions of oil and gas companies' direct role in exacerbating the climate crisis.
- Facilitated an attempted investor-led climate resolution at TotalEnergies. We offered a coalition of 11 institutional investors guidance on drafting a resolution text and supported procedural activities in bringing a Paris-alignment resolution to the table at the company. When the company's board unilaterally blocked the resolution, we worked to push the envelope on what is acceptable company behaviour and commenced ground-breaking work to advocate for shareholder rights in France – this has opened doors for us to change stakeholder sentiments. On invitation, we amplified the message by commenting publicly before the Paris Stock Exchange Committee. We hope that our work in France will have a legacy like that of our pioneering climate resolutions in the US.
- Experienced immense organizational growth that makes us confident that we have readied ourselves for an impactful 2023. The geopolitical context presented many challenges to our work and meant that we needed to take stock of our approach. As a result, we revised our strategy and theory of change, developing our repertoire of escalation tactics, taking a strategic company focus for the coming season. Since, we have renewed our focus on calling investors in and we were able to secure institutional investors with a total of 1.3 trillion euros in assets as co-filers for our resolutions for the 2023 AGM season.

The long chain of responsibility

Despite the constant challenges that businesses face, not least from shareholder activists, there is a level of public trust that remains. This provides a valuable opportunity to help drive change.

The Edelman Trust Barometer, an annual survey that measures the level of trust people have in various institutions, such as government, media, businesses and non-governmental organisations (NGOs), brings together findings from around the world.

According to the 2023 Trust Barometer:

> A lack of faith in societal institutions triggered by economic anxiety, disinformation, mass-class divide, and a failure of leadership has brought us to where we are today – deeply and dangerously polarized.

- Business is the only institution seen as competent and ethical.
- Fifty-three percent of respondents globally say that their countries are more divided today than in the past.
- CEOs are obligated to improve economic optimism and hold divisive forces accountable.[15]

Actually, the figures put business only just ahead of NGOs illustrating the importance of activists as well. That suggests that NGOs and businesses together secure change that will be trusted. Whereas the media and government lack that trust.

According to the same 2023 report, consumers and employees pressure business to stand up for them. It cites an earlier report by the firm that found a high number of respondents, 63%, that claimed 'I buy or advocate for brands based on my beliefs and values'. It also found that 69% of respondents claimed that 'Having societal impact is a strong expectation or deal breaker when considering a job'.[16]

But those who support businesses, such as Edelman, are also being targeted. The pressure is being applied across the entire supply chain for a business. Edelman has, for instance, faced criticism for the types of clients that it works for and for some of the campaigns in which it has been involved.

None of this reduces the important role that the Trust Barometer plays but it does demonstrate that no company is immune from being challenged. Edelman's work for oil and gas companies has been highlighted by Greenpeace;[17] scientists have called on them, and others, to stop working for fossil fuel clients.[18] Edelman has also faced criticism for its work in the Middle East, for instance with Saudi Arabia.

A number of PR firms have demonstrated that they will not work for fossil fuel companies by signing the Clean Creatives Pledge. As of January 2024, those signed up include 860 agencies and 2,000 creatives.

> Clean Creatives is bringing together leading agencies, their employees, and clients to address the ad and PR industry's work with fossil fuels. Continuing to work for fossil fuel companies poses risks to brands that prioritize sustainability, and their agencies.

The Clean Creatives pledge is the best way to show you are committed to a future for the creative industry that doesn't include promoting pollution.

As creatives or leaders of agencies, the pledge says that you will decline future contracts with the fossil fuel industry.

As clients, it says you will decline work with agencies that retain fossil fuel industry clients.[19]

The more that PR and other firms in a supply chain take action, the more scrutiny will be applied to others. The behaviour of the client base of firms will come under even greater scrutiny. Clean Creatives have campaigned hard themselves to focus on the likes of Edelman, and others, highlighting who their clients are and the activities they are engaged in.

Oil and gas companies have not been helped by evidence about the extent to which they were aware of the damage they were doing to the climate before it was ever admitted in public. Activists are, in effect, trying to show that, just as tobacco companies knew about the health damage their products inflicted and tried to cover it up, oil and gas companies did the same with climate change. Nothing illustrates a lack of trust in oil companies more than BP's weakening of its climate targets. Whilst the company leadership have justified the need to move away from the targets, it has undermined faith in the company and met with a substantial backlash from activists.[20] This was even more the case because of the way that Bernard Looney, on his appointment as BP's Chief Executive, appeared committed to tackling climate change and embodied a new approach. The sense of disappointment was palpable.

In the *Science* report, 'Assessing ExxonMobil's global warming projections', the abstract states:

Their projections were also consistent with, and at least as skilful as, those of independent academic and government models. Exxon and ExxonMobil Corp also correctly rejected the prospect of a coming ice age, accurately predicted when human-caused global warming would first be detected, and reasonably estimated the 'carbon budget' for holding warming below 2°C. On each of these points, however, the company's public statements about climate science contradicted its own scientific data.[21]

The covering up of this type of evidence has led to lawsuits. It also provides another demonstration that problems are inevitably only ever delayed, not avoided.

The legal approach is also used to secure the release of documents that others can then use in their campaigns. Yet another example of one approach reinforcing another in an activist's campaign.

Reflections

Activists are increasingly aware of the range of opportunities open to them. Technology has undoubtedly helped and has democratised a range of legal options, alongside others. By being able to, for instance, spread the costs involved in share ownership or legal challenges, activists have more options available to them.

Much of this chapter has focused on domestic opportunities but the reality is that activists look to the level of government or legal redress that works for their aims. That could be the OECD, World Bank, COP, United Nations, World Health Organization, etc.

Activists are always looking for new ways to apply pressure. That also includes through legal redress.

As has been discussed throughout the book, a gap can emerge between the fantastic words in a company or government announcement, and the subsequent delivery. An eye-catching announcement may reassure stakeholders, gain media attention or spread across social media, but it always needs to be followed-up on and, ultimately, delivered.

If not, then that leaves a gap now for not just reputational damage but also potential legal challenge. Shareholder activism looks for new ways to ensure the good management of companies. The rise of 'overboarding' has become part of their arguments. This is when directors, especially non-executive directors, hold so many board positions that it could be argued they cannot possibly fulfil their intended roles effectively.[22]

This chapter has shown how the legal system is being increasingly used as a tool for activists, whether targeting businesses or governments. Favourable judicial rulings are of huge benefit to activists in making an immediate impact in helping to change behaviour, but also have a catalysing impact on motivating others, raising funds and garnering attention. But even adverse findings may not be the end of the world either.

Businesses should be used to the idea that every aspect of their operations are liable to legal challenges – shareholder litigation, regulatory investigations into 'greenwashing', and community-funded litigation around issues such as environmental harm mean that businesses have to be increasingly vigilant. Under those circumstances, it can be argued, the activists have already made a significant breakthrough.

There is no excuse for business leaders not to recognise the power of the law, and research, such as that from FTI mentioned at the start of this chapter, suggests areas where businesses can expect challenges to come from. They should be paying attention to the examples going on around them as well.

The threat of legal action can put businesses on the defensive and force them to carefully consider their public commitments and messaging around, for instance, ESG issues. The law is becoming a tool to hold companies accountable and place them under intense public scrutiny but also with specific audiences as well. Ones that could have a significant impact on operations, sales, business relationships, etc. With that scrutiny comes pressure and the threat of significant consequences.

As businesses appear to be becoming aware of the lack of consistency around ESG measures, increasing numbers of voluntary commitments, different standards between countries and divergences between businesses all provide avenues for activist challenges, including through the legal system. Corporate commitments to standards, of various types, create expectations, statements and a paper trail, all of which activists can look to utilise.

For activists, the law is no longer the preserve of well-funded corporates, and they do not need to feel at a disadvantage. It may be 'David vs Goliath' in terms of size, but not in terms of the ability to use the law.

The strategic use of the law goes beyond the courtroom. A legal action can serve a valuable role in broader public campaigns, securing media attention, motivating supporters, maintaining profile, and bringing political pressure. Whilst a legal win would be the best outcome for a challenge, it is not always necessary. That means that the use of the law is a means to an end, rather than an end in itself.

The use of the law looks set to intensify still further. If behaviours such as 'greenwashing' are on the rise then activists, governments and regulators will all be considering their legal options. Businesses need to factor all aspects of their behaviours and operations into how others could challenge them legally.

Ultimately, the use of the law appears to provide a further indicator that areas of activism are not distinct but are instead fertile ground for cross-pollination, all serving the aims of the campaign. Businesses that fail to recognise this will struggle to respond.

Notes

1 Rob Mindell, Dan Healy, and Jack Hickman, 'The decade of disputes: Spotlight on environmental litigation' 19 April 2023, https://fticommunications.com/the-decade-of-disputes-spotlight-on-environmental-litigation/

2 Isabella Kaminski, 'Why 2023 will be a watershed year for climate litigation', *The Guardian*, 4 January 2023, www.theguardian.com/environment/2023/jan/04/why-2023-will-be-a-watershed-year-for-climate-litigation#:~:text=Early%20this%20year%2C%20the%20UN,negative%20impacts%20of%20climate%20change

3 Janice Hopkins Tanne, 'US Supreme Court ends constitutional right to abortion', *The BMJ*, 377 (June 2022), www.bmj.com/content/377/bmj.o1575

4 Pew Research Center, 'Public opinion on abortion', fact sheet, 17 May 2022, www.pewresearch.org/religion/fact-sheet/public-opinion-on-abortion/

5 See www.crowdjustice.com

6 Mia Gomez, *Biography of Thomas Boone Pickens, Jr. (1928–2019)*, Texas State Historical Association, www.tshaonline.org/handbook/entries/pickens-thomas-boone-jr

7   Lazard, 'Annual review of shareholder activism 2023', 8 January 2024, www.laza rd.com/research-insights/annual-review-of-shareholder-activism-2023/

8   Victor Barros, Maria João Guedes, Joana Santos, and Joaquim Miranda Sarmento, 'Shareholder activism and firms' performance', *Research in International Business and Finance*, 64 (January 2023), www.sciencedirect.com/science/article/pii/S027553192200246X

9   S. Rafaqat, S. Rafaqat, S. Rafaqat, S. Rafaqat and D. Rafaqat, 'Shareholder activism and firm performance: A review', *Journal of Economics and Behavioral Studies*, 14(4J) (2022), pp. 31–41

10 ClientEarth, 'Five leading shareholder actions', 7 April 2022, www.clientearth. org/latest/news/5-leading-shareholder-actions/

11 See https://corpgov.law.harvard.edu

12 Ashley Armstrong, 'Billionaire activist Nelson Peltz takes seat on Unilever's board', *The Times*, 1 June 2022, www.thetimes.co.uk/article/billionaire-activist-nelson-peltz-takes-seat-on-unilevers-board-0n5nv2hm3

13 Paul Verney, 'VW publishes climate lobbying report following investor pressure', *Responsible Investor*, 4 May 2023, www.responsible-investor.com/vw-publishes-climate-lobbying-report-following-investor-pressure/

14 For a full description see Follow This website, www.follow-this.org

15 Edelman Trust Barometer 2023, 'Navigating a polarized world', 2023, www. edelman.com/trust/2023/trust-barometer

16 Edelman Trust Barometer 2023, 'Navigating a polarized world', 2023, www. edelman.com/trust/2023/trust-barometer

17 Jesse Colman, 'Leaked: What you should know about Edelman and TransCanada's attack plan', 20 November 2014, www.greenpeace.org/usa/leaked-edelman-transcanadas-pr-attack-plan/

18 Steven Mufson, 'More than 450 scientists call on PR and ad firms to cut their ties with fossil fuel clients', *Washington Post*, 19 January 2022, www.washingtonpost.com/climate-environment/2022/01/19/pr-firms-fossil-fuels-climate/

19 For full details see https://cleancreatives.org

20 Emily Gosden, 'Invest in oil or risk the green future, warns BP boss', *The Times*, 1 March 2023, www.thetimes.com/business-money/article/invest-in-oil-or-risk-the-green-future-warns-bp-boss-lr7cbwbf8

21 G. Suprna, S. Rahmstorf and N. Oreskes, 'Assessing ExxonMobil's global warming projections', *Science*, 379(6628) (January 2023), www.science.org/doi/10.1126/science.abk0063

22 Working It podcast, '"Overboarding": The perils of sitting on too many boards', *Financial Times*, 7 March 2023, www.ft.com/content/ed7c019e-3e87-4b49-b14e-97a5c9e79afa

Chapter 5

The business fightback
Attempts to build immunity

Businesses are starting to use a range of tactics to try to protect themselves from attacks. Unfortunately for them, many activists have public sympathy on their side and often know the rulebooks better than the businesses themselves. This disruption to 'business as usual' is proving highly effective. Some take genuine action. Some ignore. Others then face activist campaigns.

Some businesses have tried to undermine the campaigns themselves, often using what some would consider dubious tactics. When details become known, such as those released by Greenpeace about the targeting of critics of an oil project in Canada[1] or efforts to undermine proposed policies such as the Clean Fuel Standard,[2] then the reputational damage is greater still.

This has brought with it increased efforts to establish reputationally beneficial partnerships and relationships. Businesses work with charities on campaigns, with traditional opponents to try to solve difficult issues, and adopt prominent positions on issues to grow understanding and knowledge about them. These platforms have not always had the intended effect and have sometimes led to a backlash suggesting 'greenwashing', 'sportswashing' or similar. 'Washing' is a distraction technique.

Reputation building

The nature of some businesses means that they more regularly come into contact with campaigners. It is simply part of their operations. However, the spotlight has become broader. There is no guaranteeing that just because a business has not been the subject of a campaign before, it will not be in the future. This could come about because of their operations or behaviour. Consider how Fujitsu has become the subject of campaigning considering its actions and public comments through the Post Office Horizon scandal going back many years. What the company knew, and when and how that was communicated, is part of ongoing inquiries but has already led to senior executives having to apologise.

No organisation has an inherent right to immunity. But activist campaigns should be viewed as both a risk and an opportunity. This is not all

DOI: 10.4324/9781003371908-6

about protecting an organisation from reputational and other forms of damage. Instead, a spotlight can lead to a potentially valuable change in approach.

In the first place, it is easier to ensure that an attack is less likely to happen and that means paying attention to activists and campaigns.

There should be three stages:

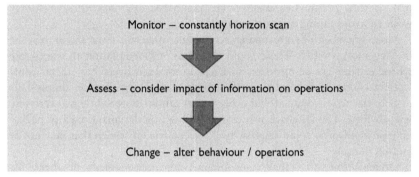

Monitor – constantly horizon scan

Assess – consider impact of information on operations

Change – alter behaviour / operations

This should be an ongoing process. If change is required, then the internal processes should already exist to make that happen. This places the emphasis on existing good internal relationships. These are not solely about the personal, although they are important, but also a good understanding of what will happen if change does not happen. That requires a full assessment of the risk and resulting impacts.

There is also a need to be clear about timescales. Any audience will want to see that progress is being made but it does not mean that delivery has to be instantaneous. Such an approach may suggest that action was easy and will raise more questions about why change did not happen earlier. Instead, an organisation needs to be open and honest about what is achievable and by when.

The real problems for an organisation emerge when they become focused on avoiding bad headlines or difficult discussions with any stakeholder group. They actively encourage a gap to emerge between the reality and the rhetoric. A potentially damaging gap between what they say they will do and what they actually do.

The bigger the 'say-do' gap, the bigger the potentially damaging implications.

Just like any political scandal is adjoined by the suffix '-gate', any organisation that is said to be making false or misleading claims about part of its operations are said to be engaged in 'washing' their reputation. It is a way of distracting from reality.

Washing up

'Greenwashing' is one of the most common 'washing' terms. It is used to describe a situation where an organisation makes a false or misleading environmental claim about their products or activities. They engage in 'greenwashing' to try to give the impression that they are acting in an environmentally friendly way. As expectations grow and Net Zero becomes the 'norm' for more organisations, the pressure to take the environment seriously increases. 'Greenwashing' may be tempting for those who feel that they are being left behind, may be losing their competitive edge, are only making slow progress especially when compared to competitors, or simply want to avoid taking any real action.

Most organisations are taking action but others in their sector may be moving more swiftly. There could then exist the temptation to exaggerate whatever they are doing to try to keep up, or even overtake, others. Some 'greenwashing' may be obvious, for instance if an organisation simply fails to take the action claimed, but other forms can be more subtle and certainly less obvious. The language used for a product, or the image used in packaging or in adverts, could suggest that it is eco-friendly when that may not in fact be the case.

Organisations find that 'outsourcing' the measurement of their, for instance, environmental measures provides a useful and independent way of demonstrating commitment and progress. This does not guarantee that mistakes will not be made but it means that a business has the confidence not to 'mark its own homework'.

However, the number of certification schemes can make it confusing, and some companies have been criticised for signing up to certification schemes that lack rigour. When Cadbury left the Fairtrade certification scheme and worked with its own in-house, Cocoa Life, it faced such criticism of lack of rigour (which it rigorously denied).

In theory, some instances of 'greenwashing' could be accidental. It may arise when over-ambitious targets are set but updates on progress not provided. Not all 'greenwashing' is a deliberate attempt to mislead. Sadly, however, whether accidental or not, it remains 'greenwashing'.

For some it can be a more deliberate attempt to mislead stakeholders, especially consumers. It tells a story of environmental protection that belies the reality of inaction. Businesses, under these circumstances, can continue their existing practices without making efforts to reduce their impact on the environment.

If any organisation is serious about avoiding accusations of 'greenwashing' then it needs to:

- keep stakeholders up to date with developments
- make information freely and readily available
- report regularly
- constantly seek to improve
- learn from the best practice of others, not just direct competitors but from other sectors as well.

There are many examples of 'greenwashing' being called out leading to changes in behaviour. Take, for example, HSBC which committed to ending the financing of the development of new oil and gas fields only months after being called out for 'greenwashing'.[3]

Concerns about 'greenwashing' are rising, so much so that the Competition and Markets Authority (CMA) in the UK launched an investigation into the 'green' claims made in advertising for basic household products including food, drinks and toiletries.[4] The CMA says it is concerned consumers are 'paying a premium for products that aren't what they seem'. The head of the CMA, Sarah Cardell, even went so far as to say that she was concerned that there could be 'greenwashing' and that 'Now is a good time for businesses to review their practices and make sure they're operating within the law'.[5] This represents a stark warning and suggests that, deliberate or otherwise, some may be breaking the law.

This is in addition to an already ongoing investigation into Asos, Boohoo and Asda as the CMA were 'concerned about the way the firms' products are being marketed to customers as eco-friendly'.[6] It also promised investigations into 'potentially misleading environmental claims in other sectors'.[7]

Having published a Green Claims Code in late 2021[8] after finding that 40% of green claims made online could be misleading,[9] the CMA is continuing to take action.

But other UK government agencies have also been moving against greenwashing and this is a growing trend across governments. Why? There are a range of reasons but not least governments often struggle to make significant changes themselves, so place the onus on others. That may be a sceptical suggestion and does not mean that good work is not taking place across government departments, agencies and at state and local levels, but many consider that the market needs to demonstrate that change can be implemented at scale.

The UK Financial Conduct Authority (FCA) issued a consultation with measures aimed at stopping greenwashing. They are considering potential new rules to protect consumers and improve trust in sustainable investment products. There has been criticism that there is a lack of clarity around the products and that it is 'too easy' to claim green credentials. Certainly, when the FCA made its announcement, it was warmly welcomed.

The FCA is proposing to introduce:

- sustainable investment product labels that will give consumers the confidence to choose the right products for them. There will be three categories – including one for products improving their sustainability over time – underpinned by objective criteria.
- restrictions on how certain sustainability-related terms – such as 'ESG', 'green' or 'sustainable' – can be used in product names and

marketing for products which don't qualify for the sustainable investment labels. It is also proposing a more general anti-greenwashing rule covering all regulated firms. This will help avoid misleading marketing of products.

- consumer-facing disclosures to help consumers understand the key sustainability-related features of an investment product – this includes disclosing investments that a consumer may not expect to be held in the product.
- more detailed disclosures, suitable for institutional investors or retail investors that want to know more.
- requirements for distributors of products, such as investment platforms, to ensure that the labels and consumer-facing disclosures are accessible and clear to consumers.[10]

Then there is the UK Advertising Standards Authority (ASA) which has been taking action again against those exaggerating green credentials or making misleading claims. Some recent examples include Ryanair, Innocent Drinks, Quorn, Shell and others.[11]

An academic study published in *Plos One*,[12] criticised the continued gap between the public pronouncements of some fossil fuel companies and their actual investment strategies. The research concluded that:

the transition to clean energy business models is not occurring, since the magnitude of investments and actions does not match discourse. Until actions and investment behaviour are brought into alignment with discourse, accusations of greenwashing appear well-founded.

The existence of that gap rightly places communications under a spotlight. Internal teams and advisers can, of course, be misled, but are they asking the right questions, receiving sufficient reassurance and getting to the heart of the activities? If not, then a question needs to be posed about whether communications are simply facilitating 'washing'.

The communications sector is therefore taking the challenge of dealing with 'greenwashing' seriously and has introduced self-regulatory measures.

Back in 2008, in a letter to *PR Week* the then chair of the CIPR Environmental Sustainability Guidelines explained what action was being taken to deal with the credibility issue facing the sector.

During our study for the CIPR we found greenwashing is not just prevalent in the corporate world, but also across government and some NGOs / pressure groups, particularly with regards to how environmental statistics are presented. It has become the new marketing opportunity for everyone.[13]

But accusations remain that the PR industry is failing to address 'greenwashing' and is contributing to its continuation and proliferation.

Similarly, the PRCA established a Climate Misinformation Strategy Group. Its second annual research report found that:

- more than nine out of ten (96%) of PR professionals now advise their clients and colleagues to understand the climate crisis and how they can effectively communicate the part they play – up from 82% the previous year.
- almost half (45%) have noticed their clients or organisation attempting to greenwash, however 89% have pushed back on this and 57% managed to change the approach as a result.
- almost all (97%) said they have taken action to address the climate crisis but only 48% measure their carbon footprint.
- 71% of consumers say they would stop buying from a brand if they knew it had misled its customers about having a positive environmental impact.[14]

This counteracts the narrative that PR is failing to take the challenge seriously and is, in some cases, collaborating to make the issue worse. This Group has now been relaunched as the Climate Communication Group with a mission to: 'help PR and communication professionals understand their responsibility when it comes to advising on climate change and how to integrate and communicate it'.[15]

That does not stop the likes of Open Democracy calling out firms for working with fossil fuel companies.[16] The comments made by the United Nations (UN) have given such scrutiny added impetus. The UN report 'Integrity Matters: Net Zero Commitments by Business, Financial Institutions, Cities and Regions' was damning in its conclusions. In a speech to the General Assembly, António Guterres, the UN Secretary-General, said:

We need to hold fossil fuel companies and their enablers to account.

That includes the banks, private equity, asset managers and other financial institutions that continue to invest and underwrite carbon pollution.

And it includes the massive public relations machine raking in billions to shield the fossil fuel industry from scrutiny.

Just as they did for the tobacco industry decades before, lobbyists and spin doctors have spewed harmful misinformation.

Fossil fuel interests need to spend less time averting a PR disaster – and more time averting a planetary one.[17]

The 'Integrity Matters' report includes potential pathways to action:

For regulators, initiatives, and standard setters as a series of critical next steps to deliver on this work. We believe that these bodies, as well as many others, can steer non-state actors to deliver with rigour, transparency, and fairness on their net zero pledges.[18]

Launching the report at COP27 in Sharm el-Sheikh, Egypt, the Secretary General said: 'We must have zero tolerance for net zero greenwashing', going on to say that promises cannot be a 'toxic cover-up'.[19] One of the report's recommendations is to say that the fight against 'greenwashing' 'means lobbying for positive climate action and not lobbying against it'.

Such analysis provides further impetus to campaigns such as that run by Clean Creatives. In September 2021, they launched 'The F-List' which detailed 90 Ad and PR agencies working with fossil fuel corporations and compared their pledges for climate action 'with their work to greenwash their clients' image and spread climate misinformation'.[20]

With the wind of the UN behind them, it is clear that activists will look to apply pressure at any point in an organisation's supply and consultancy chain.

Clean Creatives has started to apply pressure on the communications sector. It has recently focused on Edelman, largely as a result of the profile it has because of its Trust Barometer. It highlighted that the company had worked with Charles Koch, who has long challenged climate change, whilst having a commitment to not working on climate denial projects. The company has vigorously defended its position.

The idea that organisations are not just saying and doing different things but are actively campaigning, and lobbying, against possible change appears to be yet another phase of campaigning. The relationship between Koch and Edelman appears to have been revealed in tax documents – another example of how all public documents, however they are released, are critical in campaigns.

A report by InfluenceMap in December 2022, suggested that US truck manufacturers 'are actively lobbying to weaken and delay key US climate policies promoting zero-emission trucks, while simultaneously running PR campaigns that appear to promote the decarbonization of the sector'.[21]

An investigation by the US Congress House Oversight Committee into fossil fuel companies came to an end when the Republicans took control of the House of Representatives. But before that happened, the Committee had held evidence sessions and released a wide range of documents.[22] There was also an inquiry by the House Committee on Natural Resources looking at the role of PR firms in 'Preventing Action on Climate Change'.

Whilst the conclusions of the Oversight Committee work were disputed, not least by the fossil fuel companies, it was also a battleground between Democrats and Republicans. Democratic representatives Carolyn B. Maloney and Ro Khanna sent a letter to the rest of the Oversight Committee detailing what they said was the latest from the investigation into the fossil fuel industry's response to climate change. They considered that the documents received by the Committee:

demonstrate how the fossil fuel industry 'greenwashed' its public image with promises and actions that oil and gas executives knew would not meaningfully reduce emissions, even as the industry moved aggressively to lock in continued fossil fuel production for decades to come – actions that could doom global efforts to prevent catastrophic climate change.[23]

The more that politicians start to find fault, the more likely it is that action is forthcoming. That likelihood will only increase if politicians, and the companies involved themselves, come under continued pressure. That is where activists come into the equation. All these actions become self-reinforcing.

It may serve the purpose of some to suggest that activists are leading the fight. That can provide cover to governments who wish only to take action when 'forced' to or when they want to contend that a campaign represents only a narrow sectional interest or is merely a fringe concern.

But if we consider 'greenwashing' then it has gone mainstream. You cannot have the UN, congressional committees and others highlighting the challenge without it being part of the mainstream discourse.

Greenpeace has even gone so far as to suggest that we live in a 'golden age' of 'greenwashing'. For them, it is not just about the communication. They have criticised the role that 'offsetting' plays in helping organisations to avoid their environmental commitments.

> Offsetting has become the most popular and sophisticated form of greenwash around. The idea is deceptively simple: instead of cutting your own carbon emissions, you pay someone else to cut theirs or somehow capture yours. In theory, this mechanism could work since it doesn't matter where in the world the carbon is emitted as long as the same quantity is taken out of the atmosphere somewhere else. In practice, though, offsetting is riddled with flaws.[24]

Other reports too provide examples of what could, at the very least, be described as poor behaviour. The UK Climate Change Committee issued 'The role of transition plans in the UK's pathway to Net Zero' in May 2022 to consider the role that transition plans play, how they can be governed and monitored, etc. The Committee was considering organisations that have expressed commitment to the Net Zero agenda and have, it appears, put plans of action in place to deliver on those commitments. However, the report concluded that: 'A number of organisations have published frameworks for transition plans, but these set out different visions of what it should contain and how it will be structured'.[25]

The Committee sees real benefit in transition plans but worries that they may not be sufficiently transparent or comprehensive. It suggests ways in which transition plans can reassure audiences, not least that there should be 'a level of independent assurance of transition plans, to address green-washing concerns'.[26]

In other words, even when plans do exist many are sadly lacking. The Committee has set out what they expect so organisations know what they need to deliver. That is the fundamental challenge.

Pushing the boundaries

There are many examples of companies who are only, it appears, too willing to push the boundaries of what they say and what they do to the very edge of what is acceptable and maybe even beyond (both in terms of public attitude and potentially even legally). This sadly undermines trust and does little to reassure audiences about business efforts.

In *Reputation in Business: Lessons for Leaders* (Routledge, 2023), I mentioned the fast fashion brand BooHoo and the issues they have encountered regarding their use of labour. By the time of this book, they are being investigated by the CMA, as mentioned above.

As the CMA states, it 'is concerned about the way the firms' products are being marketed to customers as eco-friendly' and 'the investigation will scrutinise environmental claims made by ASOS, Boohoo and George at Asda about their fashion products, including clothing, footwear, and accessories'.[27]

The CMA investigation will consider issues around statements and language used, what is included in product ranges, a lack of information to customers, and potentially misleading claims about accreditation schemes used.

That is not to say that BooHoo have not attempted to make strides in the last year, but they continue to be the subject of significant media scrutiny.[28] Some writers have claimed that the 'fast fashion' industry as a whole has a sustainability issue,[29] but at least BooHoo has engaged with Kourtney Kardashian to help them move along their sustainability journey.[30]

It is not just fast fashion that is coming under fire. The CMA are also looking at fast moving consumer goods, as their Chief Executive said: 'We're concerned many shoppers are being misled and potentially even paying a premium for products that aren't what they seem'.

Both investigations form part of a work stream into 'misleading green claims', i.e. 'greenwashing'. The CMA's Green Claims Code,[31] to help business avoid such an approach, does not seem to be having sufficient impact, so action may be taken against those who continue to mislead consumers.

It is clear that the CMA considers that there is a problem which needs to be looked at. It would be wrong to pre-empt the outcome of any investigations, but regulatory bodies are on the lookout for gaps between what companies say they or their products do, and what they actually do.

Regulators often have real investigation and prosecution powers, so the consequences for businesses when they get involved are not confined to some poor publicity. They can enter buildings, seize information, demand papers – all this creates its own reputational damage.

An organisation also needs to consider the impact on its day-to-day as well. An investigation can take years. It takes up time and resources. Regulators may publish initial findings and then a final report. The huge implications for operations as well as in reputational terms should not be underestimated. That is to say nothing of the powers around criminal prosecutions that some regulators have as well.

As a general rule of thumb, regulators in the US have more teeth, but the trend elsewhere is in this direction. Governments like to be seen to be 'beefing up' regulators so that they can protect consumers. Some argue that this is regulatory creep but for others it is the consequence of the need to protect consumers more fully.

The fundamental foundation of reputation remains the same. Where the gap appears, trouble is likely.

The UK government too implicitly sees 'greenwashing' as a problem. The establishment of an independent expert advisory group in June 2021 to 'support investors, consumers and businesses to make green financial decisions'[32] shows that it wants to be seen as tackling the problem.

The Green Technical Advisory Group will 'provide independent, non-binding advice to the Government on developing and implementing a green taxonomy in the UK context'. The Government sees the work of the group as contributing to a boost investment to help the transition to a sustainable economy, the creation of green jobs and to support the UK's overall environmental goals.

The Green Technical Advisory Group will oversee the Government's delivery of a 'Green Taxonomy' – 'a common framework setting the bar for investments that can be defined as environmentally sustainable'.

As things stand, as a consequence of Brexit, the UK is not part of the EU's green taxonomy plans. However, it is promising action of its own, although its original timeline for action has not been met.

The membership of the group includes business groups, taxonomy and data experts, users of taxonomy, academics but also NGOs. Government recognises that a broad range of views are required if the work of the group, and its advice, is to have any effect.

The US government too is facing calls to take action against 'greenwashing'. Using the same CMA-led data about the numbers of companies involved in 'greenwashing', the International Consumer Protection and Enforcement Network wants the Biden administration to move against poor practice.[33]

The administration has suggested that new climate change units could be created in agencies such as the Treasury Department, Federal Reserve, Commodity Futures Trading Commission and the SEC.

The SEC has adopted a more robust approach to regulation and enforcement around ESG issues. It has taken action against both US and non-US companies for 'greenwashing'. The SEC has recently taken action against US and non-US companies for 'greenwashing', and it is working on new disclosure requirements for public companies as well as investment managers and funds. In March 2021, it set up a Climate and ESG Task Force:

> Consistent with increasing investor focus and reliance on climate and ESG-related disclosure and investment, the Climate and ESG Task Force will develop initiatives to proactively identify ESG-related misconduct. The task force will also coordinate the effective use of Division resources, including through the use of sophisticated data analysis to mine and assess information across registrants, to identify potential violations.[34]

There has already been action against a US investment manager and a non-US mining company. But different arguments often resonate with different governments. The complaints made by the likes of Patagonia have suggested that companies that take the environment seriously are struggling to contend with the 'greenwashing' of others.

This creates challenges for those that genuinely want to deliver for the environment – for companies, they need to know who they can do business with, and consumers want to know who they can buy from. So, commercially, this is a problem that many consider needs to be tackled. 'Greenwashing' distorts competition.

Larry Fink, the Chief Executive of BlackRock called for more disclosure in his 2021 annual letter to CEOs:

> Given how central the energy transition will be to every company's growth prospect, we are asking companies to disclose a plan for how their business model will be compatible with a net zero economy – that is, one where global warming is limited to well below 2°C, consistent with a global aspiration of net zero greenhouse gas emissions by 2050. We are asking you to disclose how this plan is incorporated into your long-term strategy and reviewed by your board of directors.[35]

And:

> We strongly support moving to a single global standard, which will enable investors to make more informed decisions about how to achieve durable long-term returns.[36]

By 2022, he was focusing clearly on leadership:

> It's never been more essential for CEOs to have a consistent voice, a clear purpose, a coherent strategy, and a long-term view...

> Every company and every industry will be transformed by the transition to a net zero world. The question is, will you lead, or will you be led?

And appreciating the commercial side of protecting the environment:

> We focus on sustainability not because we're environmentalists, but because we are capitalists and fiduciaries to our clients...
>
> Capitalism has the power to shape society and act as a powerful catalyst for change.

And to secure change needs public and private to work together:

> When we harness the power of both the public and private sectors, we can achieve truly incredible things. This is what we must do to get to net zero...
>
> That's why we are launching a Center for Stakeholder Capitalism, to create a forum for research, dialogue, and debate. It will help us to further explore the relationships between companies and their stakeholders and between stakeholder engagement and shareholder value. We will bring together leading CEOs, investors, policy experts, and academics to share their experience and deliver their insights.[37]

Stakeholder capitalism is nothing new, but it appears that Fink considers the challenges of the current era so critical that joint working is required.

Advertising

Advertising is a very clear way in which businesses communicate directly with the public. Regulators dealing with advertising have been particularly busy considering 'greenwashing'. Advertising can be at the forefront of delivering clarity or potentially obscuring a company's true actions.

The UK's ASA has, for instance, taken the following action:

- Ryanair – considered a campaign by the airline which claimed the company had 'low CO_2 emissions' and was the 'lowest emissions airline'. The ASA criticised the latter as it was based on a study from around a decade before and failed to sufficiently justify the claim.
- Lufthansa – banned a poster because it included a link to a marketing website that included misleading claims.
- Innocent Drinks – found that an animated ad that drew an association between the drinks and a positive impact on the environment was misleading.

- Quorn – found that environmental claims in a product ad were misleading because they did not clear the basis of the claims.
- Shell – decided that a loyalty programme being advertised was misleading because it was not clear that it was a carbon offsetting scheme rather than a new carbon neutral fuel that could deliver the promise to 'drive carbon neutral'.
- HSBC – complaints about two posters were upheld because of unclear environmental claims that required more information to be provided.

This demonstrates that even those organisations that really understand the need to make progress towards net zero can still make mistakes. HSBC has been explicit about the damage likely to come about if it is not clear about its progress on net zero:

> We have considered the impact of climate-related issues on our businesses, strategy, and financial planning. Our access to capital may be impacted by reputational concerns as a result of climate action or inaction. In addition, if we are perceived to mislead stakeholders on our business activities or if we fail to achieve our stated net zero ambitions, we could face greenwashing risk resulting in significant reputational damage, impacting our revenue generating ability and potentially our access to capital.[38]

But the ASA finding has not been the only misstep for the company: HSBC Asset Management's then Global Head of Responsible Investment, Stuart Kirk, moved on from his job after a speech at a *Financial Times* conference saying 'why investors need not worry about climate risk'.[39] The senior leadership team quickly tried to put space between themselves and Kirk. He defended his position through a LinkedIn post.[40]

The bank's own report sees the real spectre of reputational damage if clarity is not central to their operations. But being as aware is not the same as ensuring that all aspects of an organisation, its culture and people act and behave in line with those aims.

The UK advertising regulator is not alone in combatting 'greenwashing'. The New Zealand ASA Complaints Board considered an ad by natural gas distributor Firstgas Group that claimed that its gas 'is going zero carbon'. As no details were provided, the Board believed it to be an unsubstantiated environmental claim. The complaint was made by Lawyers for Climate Action NZ who commented that:

> A huge part of the transition to a zero-carbon economy is allowing consumers to make low emissions choices. If businesses mislead consumers about how green their products are, they take away consumers' ability to make an informed choice.[41]

The Board also found that the clothing company Kathmandu were potentially in breach of their Code in the advert for a biodegradable puffer jacket. The company settled the complaint and removed the advert.

Again, global bodies have been brought into these disputes as well as complaints filed with National Contact Points (NCPs) under the OECD Guidelines for Multinational Enterprises. Each Government that adheres to the Guidelines are required to set up an NCP.

The role of the NCP is 'to further the effectiveness of the Guidelines by undertaking promotional activities, handling enquiries, and contributing to the resolution of issues that may arise from the alleged non-observance of the guidelines in specific instances'.[42] According to the OECD 2020 Annual Report, it was 'the record year in terms of cases received'.[43]

Examples of cases considered by NCPs include:

- Grupa OLX and the Frank Bold Foundation – agreement was reached over adverts that could mislead consumers.
- WWF International and Soco International Plc – action was taken to protect a World Heritage site from being damaged.[44]

Changes in regulations need to be considered across jurisdictions. The European Union in 2020 introduced a new Taxonomy Regulation that set out four overarching conditions that an economic activity has to meet in order to qualify as environmentally sustainable. The Regulation, a cornerstone of the European Green Deal, is part of the attempt to get more investment into sustainable projects, assets and companies.[45]

Activists themselves had undertaken some highly effective advertising. #Subvertising, which creates parodies of adverts or revises them to subvert their messages, can bring ridicule on corporates. It has also been used as a way of reclaiming public spaces from corporates as well. A recent example was led by Brandalism and focused on showing up the green claims made by car manufacturers.[46]

One of the most consistently impactful and high-profile groups which has used adverts and videos has been Led By Donkeys[47] whose social media biographies start by saying 'Art, activism and accountability'.[48] They have displayed tweets on billboards, projected videos onto buildings and have had banners displayed at rallies all to campaign on the issues of concern to them, particularly the fight against Brexit.

The 'hushing' challenge

Whilst some companies are being looked at for over-stating their environmental credentials, others are keeping quiet about what they are up to. 'Green hushing' is the concept that companies feel unable to talk about their achievements and plans because of the fear of reputational damage.

In its 2022 Net Zero report, South Pole, a climate consultancy, found that:

- one in four companies surveyed have set science-based emission reduction targets, but they do not plan to publicise them.
- while corporate greenwash has been widely reported, this research reveals another emerging practice among companies: 'greenhushing'.
- customer pressure and brand leadership remain the top two drivers for setting a net zero target, but findings suggest that target-setting could become an essential, not exceptional, reputational strategy for companies.
- despite this, three-quarters of all surveyed companies have increased their net zero budgets over the past year and even a majority of those not on track to meet their net zero goals are expanding their sustainability teams.[49]

Companies may choose a 'green hushing' approach because they do not want to draw attention to their environmental plans or because they do not want to highlight their impact and the scale of the task at hand. They may also though be wary of being criticised for failing to keep their environmental promises.

'Green hushing' can be thought of as a negative practice as well because it is fundamentally based on a lack of transparency and accountability. If consumers are not aware of a company's environmental efforts, or lack of them, then how can they make informed decisions about the products they purchase or the companies they deal with? Additionally, without public pressure, companies may not feel the need to prioritise environmental sustainability in their operations.

Some companies may not be actively 'hushing', preferring instead to focus on securing progress rather than communicating. Others may feel that they are still in a planning phase or that it is too early to communicate.

In a report, The Greenwashing Hydra,[50] by financial think tank Planet Tracker, they consider 'greenhushing' to refer to: 'corporate management teams under-reporting or hiding their sustainability credentials in order to evade investor scrutiny'.

They point to moves by asset management firms downgrading a number of Article 9 (dark green) funds, under Sustainable Finance Disclosure Regulation, to Article 8 (light green) funds to comply with the stricter regulations but suggest it was 'potentially undertaken to avoid the scrutiny associated with the Article 9 standard'.

The report also identifies five other types of 'greenwashing', so six in total:

- Greencrowding – hiding in a crowd to avoid discovery.
- Greenlighting – when company communications highlight a green feature in order to draw attention away from other environmentally damaging activities.

- Greenshifting – when companies imply that the consumer is at fault and shift the blame on to them.
- Greenlabelling – a practice where marketers call something green or sustainable, but on closer examination this is shown to be misleading.
- Greenrinsing – refers to a company regularly changing its ESG targets before they are achieved.

Some forms of 'greenwashing' could be considered more cynical than others. The reality is, whether deliberate or accidental, real damage to a reputation can be inflicted and, as shown, direct regulatory intervention may follow.

We can see from examples of 'greenwashing' that they seem to be based around a number of failings:

- Lack of information – claims made but unexplained.
- Lack of basis – claims made but with no meaningful justification.
- Better than others – simply positioning the product as better than others on the market.
- Non-disclosure – considering one environmental aspect of a product but not its totality.
- Misleading terms – using language which may suggest environmental benefits that do not really exist.
- Lying – simply trying to get away with it...

If failings keep happening, then regulators will feel under pressure to increase the scope of their action or may be given enhanced powers by their government to address the issue. Continued market failures ultimately lead to bigger fines and even criminal prosecution. If lying becomes the norm, or is perceived to be increasing, then the chances of action increase significantly.

Ultimately, transparency and accountability are key to promoting environmental sustainability. Consumers have the power to demand more transparency from companies and to support those that prioritise sustainability. Meanwhile, companies can benefit from being more transparent about their environmental initiatives, as it can help to build trust and loyalty with consumers.

Silence can itself eventually bring scrutiny. Adopting this strategy may offer some immediate benefits of others being in the spotlight, but in the longer term it will not work.

There is no guaranteeing that others in the sector, and especially direct competitors, will take the same approach. It is easy to become an outlier and, as such, the focus of activists, consumers and other stakeholders will eventually arrive.

It does though present the opportunity for an organisation to plan and implement before communicating more widely. In other words, an organisation must do something with the time it has available and act. It should not be considered time to hide away. Long-term silence brings scrutiny, it does not avoid it.

Research from Sensu Insight, '50 Shades of Greenwashing', shows that the public want greater transparency and there is considerable suspicion about ESG claims.[51] But there was a welcome defence of ESG from the Chief Executive of Mars, Poul Weihrauch, who criticised those who backed away from it in the face of political attacks.[52] In particular, he highlighted the potential impact on alienating a new generation of talent. In other words, companies that back down are taking a huge risk with their future prospects.

A discussion on Tessa Wernink's podcast, 'What If We Get It Right', highlights how employee activism can take a number of forms.[53] It urges businesses not to downplay ESG and notes evidence, such as a report from KPMG, that employees, especially younger ones, leave roles if employers fail to deliver on ESG.[54] The expectations of these employees towards their employers have changed. But equally if employers decide that they wish to take a more activist approach, possibly to keep these younger workers, protect themselves against the prospect of failing to attract talent in future, or maybe because they really do believe in the cause, then the employees sometimes need protection for any potential backlash from those who disagree with their activist position.[55]

There is a lot of ground to be made up.

Sportswashing

'Greenwashing' is only one way that organisations may seek to mislead. Some tactics may be directed at trying to protect their reputations as a whole rather than just considering one aspect of its operations, such as its environmental impact.

'Sportswashing' is a term is used to describe the practice of a company or a country using sports teams, events, or initiatives to try to improve its reputation. Companies can show themselves in a more favourable light to stakeholders, and can then leverage this support for several purposes such as:

- attracting inward investment
- maintaining existing investment and operations
- avoiding the removal of operations
- avoiding sanctions
- attracting workers
- distracting from specific poor behaviours or those considered unacceptable by others
- enhancing national pride.

To achieve such aims a company borrows the popularity and reputation of a sport, a sports team or tournament. This investment puts them in a more positive light. Any time that sport, team or tournament is mentioned, the links helps them to be considered more favourably.

'Sportswashing' appears to be becoming more common, and has taken on a new resonance with the influx of money from the Middle East into football and golf, but China's investment in football reaching a peak around 2016/17 illustrates that it is nothing new. Others have also suggested that hosting events such as the Football World Cup or the Olympics has provided a similar ability to wash in the past as well.

The launch of LIV Golf[56] has had major ramifications across the sport. Its mission is to: 'modernize and supercharge the wonderful sport of golf'. It also says that:

> Our events represent an opportunity to revitalize and reinvigorate golf, while helping to bring new audiences to the game. Golf is a sport full of existing traditions. The LIV Golf League intends to create new ones through our innovative and transformational approach. We believe our new format will bring fans closer to the game and generate fresh levels of excitement for the sport. And we'll complement this using our social programs that are designed to change millions of young lives across the globe for the better.

Its leadership team includes probably one of the most famous golfers of all time, and leading businessperson, Greg Norman. It organises a leading, competitive golfing competition but also has a strong commitment to supporting communities. Its charitable activity features heavily on its website as a way of demonstrating that contribution.

What is less clear from the website is that the initiative is backed by the Public Investment Fund, the sovereign wealth fund of Saudi Arabia.

Particularly in the West, Saudi Arabia has been heavily criticised for its human rights record and the way it shuts down opposition, not least the killing of journalist Jamal Khashoggi which, according to a UN report,[57] was 'an extrajudicial killing for which the State of the Kingdom of Saudi Arabia is responsible'.[58]

There have been some very forceful comments about LIV Golf and its backers. Amnesty International UK's Chief Executive, Sacha Deshmukh, said:

> It's been extremely disappointing to hear a number of golf's best-known figures attempting to play down the terrible murder of Jamal Khashoggi while sidestepping the real gravity of Saudi Arabia's appalling human rights record.
>
> Rather than acting as the willing stooges of Saudi sportswashing, we'd like to see golfers at the LIV Golf Invitational speaking out about human rights abuses in Saudi Arabia. Solidarity with Saudi Arabia's

beleaguered human rights community is incredibly important and at the moment the LIV Golf series is displaying very little of this.[59]

Golfers that took part in LIV Golf initially found themselves suspended from taking part on the existing PGA Tour. It appears that this policy may be wavering for some competitions and there has been legal action by many of the parties involved. Most recently there seems to have been a rapprochement and consideration of a merger between the PGA Tour and LIV Golf.

Football is another sport that has seen major investment from the Middle East. This includes:

- Paris Saint-Germain – owned by Nasser Al-Khelaifi of Qatar.
- Manchester City – owned by Sheikh Mansour of the United Arab Emirates.
- Aston Villa – owned by Nassef Sawiris of Egypt.
- Sheffield United – owned by Abdullah bin Musaid Al Saud of Saudi Arabia.

Some of these owners have close relationships with the rulers of the countries concerned but Saudi Arabia's Public Investment Fund was only allowed to take over Newcastle United Football Club on the basis that the state would not be in charge of the club.

This is now being challenged because of the Club's Chairman, Yasir Al-Rumayyan, being described as a 'sitting Minister of the Saudi government' during the court case between LIV Golf and the PGA.

There are also a range of sponsorships in place. Emirates, Etihad Airways and Qatar Airways are just three examples who are involved in football in several countries across Europe. The apex of this approach was arguably the hosting of the football World Cup in Qatar in 2022.

It would though be wrong to suggest that this issue only relates to the Middle East. There has previously been heavy Chinese investment in football clubs as well including Aston Villa, West Bromwich Albion and Inter Milan. And it is not just football or golf, many sports have such links. Hosting a sporting event, especially one attracting the attention of the world such as the Olympic Games, has long been seen as a way of promoting an image on the global stage and to showcase political, economic, and cultural achievements.

But activists and the media have become more aware of 'sportswashing' activities, and the level of challenge has, as a result, increased. Qatar was undoubtedly challenged over the rights of foreign workers not least during the construction of the stadiums. It was challenged over the lack of rights for those from the LGBTQIA+ community and, worse still, the illegality of same-sex sexual activity.

The spotlight has also been turned on those working with such countries, such as communications companies like Edelman, not least because of their high profile annual Trust Barometer. It demonstrates that any organisation, regardless of their place in the supply chain, are fair game for scrutiny. In the case of Edelman, the 2023 Trust Barometer calls for more brand activism, more involvement by businesses in societal issues. This could, for instance, include campaigning against the lack of LGBTQIA+ rights in many Middle Eastern countries. But for Edelman themselves, the clients they work with, and, in the past, the tactics employed, have led to criticism.[60]

There is absolutely an element of tall poppy syndrome with such criticisms, but it does demonstrate that supply chains are being considered and are not immune from challenge. In all likelihood more organisations will be called out.

Purpose washing

An organisation can use other aspects of its operations to dominate attention. Purpose washing uses an organisation's purpose, mission or aim to focus the minds of stakeholders. That may be no bad thing if the purpose is genuinely embedded and runs throughout the whole organisation and the way it operates. If that is genuinely the case then the organisation should be free to talk about it, use it as a method of differentiation and provide market advantage.

However, if an organisation allows its purpose to dominate attention whilst other forms of behaviour that do not sit within the purpose are allowed to continue, then washing is taking place. Avoiding purpose washing means aligning values with internal and external behaviours and communication.[61]

To an extent, purpose washing has become 'woke washing' which focuses particularly on organisations that use social justice themes to position themselves. Again, nothing wrong with that if their actions support the communication.

Some organisations were, for instance, proud to display a black square on Instagram following the death of George Floyd but were subsequently criticised for failing to deliver on equal rights in their own organisations.

The very act of supporting a social cause in a public way has been criticised in some quarters, particularly by those on the political right. Whilst they may face a political backlash for their social actions, Richard Edelman, Chief Executive Officer of Edelman, claimed: 'This is smart business, not woke delusion'.[62]

But as can often be the case, mistakes arise because the right sorts of initial questions are not asked, scenarios not worked through, and the potential outcomes and reactions not considered.

Take the example of the Glasgow Financial Alliance for Net Zero (Gfanz). It was launched with huge media attention at COP26 in Glasgow. It is 'a global coalition of leading financial institutions committed to accelerating the decarbonization of the economy'.[63] However, a number of members have left, leading to media speculation about the reasons, including the spotlight that was placed on it by activists who criticised a lack of change in some fields of investment. Joining any such organisation requires a whole series of questions to be asked before that commitment is made.

In such cases:

- Has there been any initial internal assessment about the level of resources required to be involved?
- Does the organisation feel pressurised to join simply because others are involved?
- Has a market advantage been identified for being involved?
- Does the organisation wish to demonstrate a clear commitment to the targets being set and have the impact of these been assessed across the whole organisation?
- Would a genuine commitment provide the internal resources required?
- Would being involved and then withdrawing make the organisation more of a target for activist pressure?

These are the types of questions that anyone signing up to standards, representative groups and similar need to work through.

There are some fantastic examples of companies which are genuinely driven by purpose. This often comes from the founder of the company. It is a personal commitment that drives all aspects of the company. We think of Patagonia and the Body Shop as older examples, through to Tenzing, Divine Chocolate and Cheeky Panda more recently. A genuinely purpose-driven company is one that is guided by a mission, not simply profits. There are increasing numbers of purpose-driven companies.

Some businesses, and countries, believe that supporting high-profile academic or other public institutions can demonstrate a commitment to that cause. That could be a university, a research institute, a museum, an exhibition, etc.

Many of these institutions welcome the financial support, especially when governments have been less generous in the funds in recent years. But such support is not without criticism. That criticism comes the way of the bene-factors as well as the beneficiaries.

The issue of Chinese support for universities, particularly in the UK and US, has concerned many. They point to the lack of free speech in China, and the link caused Marco Rubio to suggest that such support for educational institutions is 'all part of Beijing's plan to overtake the United States as the world's most powerful nation'.[64]

A *Times* investigation found that 'more than 40 British universities have collaborated with institutions that have been linked to malign activities of the Chinese state'.[65] There have also been questions about how much universities rely financially on the number of Chinese students that study at the institutions.

But it is not just links with universities; the Natural History Museum also faced criticism for signing a contract with an oil company that included a clause meaning it had to refrain from making any statement that could damage the reputation of the sponsor.[66]

Such relationships have led activist group, Fossil Free London, cited in the same article, to call for all British museums and art institutions to stop signing contracts with large corporations that contain such a gagging clause. It is 'a grassroots climate action group that aims to kick fossil fuel companies and their financiers out of the UK's capital'.[67] Following criticism, the Science Museum ended a similar sponsorship arrangement.

Such relationships are being increasingly questioned. Instead of being viewed as philanthropic endeavours, the motivations that lay behind them are questioned. Not least, they are perceived as being a block on free speech. When examples of 'gagging clauses' are revealed, this simply gives weight to that feeling.

Anyone considering entering such an arrangement, on either side, really needs to consider whether the benefits outweigh the downsides and the level of transparency that is absolutely required.

Government bodies and institutions can make similar errors. The leadership of the COP28 was questioned over its links to the state-owned Abu Dhabi National Oil Company. Whilst the outcome of the talks was generally positively received, they were all the more challenging to achieve given the initial scepticism.

When 'washing' goes wrong

When any organisation is 'caught out' then it must decide how to respond. That reaction may itself be driven by the motivations behind the approach taken in the first place.

Very often, the role of activists is to spot the behaviour and call it out. That could be with the media and directly with relevant stakeholders as well. The challenge for activists is often in providing proof. This could come in the form of whistle-blowers, leaked documents, eyewitnesses, undercover investigations, footage or increasingly looking to demonstrate the gap between behaviour and stated intentions.

When such behaviours are shown up, any organisation has choices. It could vigorously defend itself and point to all the good work done and progress achieved. Most though prefer to try to learn from the mistakes. Under those circumstances an organisation will:

- recognise the issue and apologise for the failing
- launch an independent investigation to understand what went wrong and to learn lessons
- develop a resulting plan of action to ensure that it does not happen again

- implement the plan along with any cultural and people changes necessary
- monitor progress
- ensure stakeholders are kept informed about progress.

Activists may play a role in this whole process, helping to inform the change in approach. If not, then activists will be looking to place a spotlight on every step of this process. There is often a question of transparency which all involved need to consider. Legal considerations will exert their own types of pressures around transparency, but many companies use the law as an excuse to hide behind. That does little to build bridges with stakeholders.

On occasions it can be difficult to separate a 'normal' crisis from one that relates to the consequences of 'washing'. It can only really be detected in the organisation's reaction. There may have never been an original intent to 'wash', but the reaction may be enough to cause some stakeholders to doubt the original motivations of the organisation.

The slow way in which Adidas ended its partnership with Kayne West led to outcry from one of its own directors. The company took weeks to act and when the relationship was finally ended the headlines were dominated by the word 'finally', with the articles referencing public outcry and those from charities and other organisations.[68] The company found their motivations questioned and the more outrageous Kanye West's words and behaviour became the more a gap appeared between this and the firm's commitment to diversity, equality and inclusion. Widespread condemnation of West's anti-Semitic comments was even more sensitive given Adidas's German heritage.[69]

But the issues with Kayne West are not the only challenges facing Adidas. It has, for instance, been on the receiving end of a criticism about garment workers' rights including from stunt activists The Yes Men, working with Clean Clothes Campaign, which 'appointed' a new co-CEO, a Cambodian former garment worker and union leader, 'Vay Ya Nak Phoan' ('textile' in Khmer) who immediately signed the very real Pay Your Workers agreement.[70]

The use of humour can be an effective activist weapon and can prick the pomposity of some businesses which can be perceived as taking themselves very seriously.

Co-op

There is genuine commitment to change shown by many companies, but the reality is that some prefer to defer action or try to avoid it at all. Under those circumstances, distraction techniques are often deployed. But there are also examples where the commitment and operations are fundamentally linked. One such example is the Co-op. They have run some highly effective government relations campaigns of the sort that a purely profit-driven organisation is much less likely to do. I am grateful to Paul Gerrard,

Campaign, Public Affairs and Board Secretariat at the Co-op for discussing their work with me.

It could be argued that the Co-op Group is the original purpose-driven organisation and the inspiration for many others. It traces its roots back to the foundation of the Rochdale Pioneers in 1844 which marked the beginning of the modern cooperative movement.

The Pioneers designed a set of principles that remain the foundation for all 3 million cooperative enterprises around the world today. It provides an alternative structure for organisations where the emphasis is placed on members working together to achieve common goals such as creating employment opportunities, providing goods and services, and supporting their communities.

Since the work of the Pioneers, the cooperative movement has grown and expanded globally, with cooperatives operating in a wide range of sectors, including retail, agriculture, finance, housing, and energy.

Cooperatives are organised around a set of core values and principles, which include voluntary and open membership, democratic member control, member economic participation, autonomy and independence, education, training and information, and cooperation among cooperatives. These values and principles help to ensure that cooperatives operate in a way that is both socially responsible and economically sustainable.

Today, the cooperative movement is a significant force in the global economy, with millions of members and billions of dollars in assets. It continues to be a vital tool for promoting economic democracy, empowering communities, and advancing social and environmental justice. In the UK alone, the cooperative sector in 2023 had revenues of £41 billion, over 400,000 employees and 74 million individual memberships across the 7,000 co-ops.

A co-op is different from many other kinds of businesses because it is owned by its members and other co-ops, not by investors or shareholders. That means that the members have a direct say in how the business is run.

That opens some interesting opportunities for campaigning. In the case of the Co-op Group in the UK this means that they have developed highly effective campaigns of the type that others might not choose to pursue.

One such campaign was their 'Safer Colleagues, Safer Communities', that focused on tackling violence and abuse to protect Co-op colleagues.[71]

This would not necessarily be the type of campaign that other PLC or private equity operators would pursue because publicising crime in store is not a good commercial look. However, the Co-op did as its members wanted action to be taken by government and voted for them to do just that. Members saw it as an important issue for them, colleagues in stores and the communities in which they live.

However, alongside running the campaign itself, the Co-op was already investing £70m in security, crime prevention and colleague safety measures. They recognised that action would need to be taken by the Group itself before asking government for their support if any ask was to have credibility. Again, the organisation had the ability to do that because of the direction provided by its members.

The first iteration of the campaign itself lasted nearly four years and included the following:

- Intensive support for Usdaw's, one of Britain's largest trade unions, 'Respect for Shop Workers Week' between 2018 and 2020, which included hosting hundreds of MPs in stores which allowed parliamentarians to hear about the issue of violence direct from shopworkers (and voters!) in their constituency. In 2019 this included a joint launch summit addressed by the Mayor of London, Sadiq Khan, which was attended by over 70 people from other Co-op societies, 30 leading businesses and the police.
- Inviting a number of Police and Crime commissioners into stores to encourage them to include retail crime in their local crime plans.
- Supporting very publicly, in October 2018, David Hanson MP's amendments to the Offensive Weapons Bill, which aimed to make attacks on shop workers who are selling age-restricted goods an offence that would carry heavier sentences.
- Providing opportunities for colleagues and members to petition their local MP to support the amendments.
- Targeted engagement with over 60 MPs, sending them a tailored, con-stituency-specific briefing ahead of a parliamentary debate led by David Hanson MP.
- Responding to a call for evidence from the Home Office asking for the views to aid their understanding of the problem of violence and abuse towards shop staff in England and Wales. The Co-op encouraged colleagues to respond to this call for evidence and, critically, to share their stories.
- Submitting ten recommendations to Government on how the issue could be addressed.
- Sending an open letter to all the political parties during the 2019 General Election asking them to take violence and abuse against shopwor-kers seriously.
- Media relations activity including the Co-op's Retail Chief Executive appearing on every major broadcast channel including the BBC Break-fast sofa alongside front-line colleagues.
- Commissioning Dr Emmeline Taylor to produce research on both the impact of violence on shop workers and the motivations of offenders. It shows that this abuse is having lasting effects on the lives of workers, both mentally and physically. The research shows that because of the frequency of violence and abuse, shopworkers are now suffering from post-traumatic stress disorder (PTSD).[72] The results were launched in Parliament and in the media in 2019.
- Publishing a follow-up by Dr Taylor which demonstrated how the government could legislate to protect and support shopworkers.[73]

Having colleagues brave enough to provide their own accounts and to appear across the media to talk about it as well appears to have been critical in securing government support. The Co-op worked with Matt Vickers MP directly and it was his cross-party backed amendment to the Police, Crime, Sentencing and Courts Bill in the summer of 2021 which resulted in the Government U-turning on their position and legislating to make attacking those serving the public, including shopworkers, or providing a public duty an aggravated offence in 2022.

Another example of the type of campaign that a strictly commercial body may not consider but the Co-op was able to pursue focused on tackling modern slavery, and specifically supporting victims and survivors of slavery.

The Co-op has a long history of addressing social injustice and supporting workers' rights, so this campaign was completely consistent with that. Indeed, it was the founders of the Co-operative Wholesale Society – which is now the Co-op Group – who were behind the stand the working people of Manchester took against slavery in the midst of the American Civil War, which President Lincoln called an act of heroism 'unknown in any age or country'.

Modern slavery continues to be a huge problem around the world, not just the UK. The term refers to the various forms of exploitation that involve the control or ownership of one person by another, often for the purpose of labour or sexual exploitation. It is a violation of human rights. Modern slavery encompasses a range of practices, including forced labour, debt bondage, forced marriage, human trafficking, and child labour. Victims of modern slavery may be recruited or kidnapped and then forced to work in conditions of slavery, often in sectors such as agriculture, mining, manufacturing and domestic work. They may be subjected to physical and emotional abuse, restricted movement and denial of basic human rights.

Modern slavery is a global issue affecting millions of people, with estimates suggesting that there are around 50 million people living in some form of modern slavery worldwide in 2021. It is often linked to poverty, conflict and social inequality.

The Co-op Group campaign between 2017 and 2020 including awareness-raising through partnerships with major media organisations like *The Sun* as well as through its own membership base and its business network of suppliers. In supporting legislative change, the Co-op worked with Global Citizen to create a real movement in the UK that saw a petition handed to 10 Downing Street by the leading slavery charities alongside the Co-op.

Most importantly, the Co-op created the world's biggest employment programme for slavery survivors of its kind in the world – called Bright Future – which brought together not only every major slavery charity in the UK but also more than 20 businesses who provided permanent employment for survivors. Bright Future saw the Co-op invited to present to a major UN Women conference in New York and become the first British business to be recognised with the global Thomson Reuters Stop Slavery Award in 2018.

The work of the Co-op Group shows what can be achieved by a truly purpose-driven organisation, one that lives by its principles. It is an example to others involved in campaigning, businesses of all types and particularly to other co-ops and those with alternative corporate structures such as B-corps.

When it comes to expectations the Co-op Group has set a standard by which others could be measured. If the Co-op Group can undertake such campaigning, then why can't others? If they are not undertaking campaigns, then why not? Stakeholders, not least political audiences, will come to expect similar activism from others.

That is not to say that co-ops never have issues or crises to deal with, but the key drivers of activity change the dynamic of the way they operate. This should help to minimise the chances of crises and, if one does happen, then the organisation has a strong reputation amongst stakeholders upon which to rely.

Co-ops are also used to working with others, in collaboration and partnership, because this is fundamental to the way in which they operate. Again, that delivers some level of protection from risk. There is more opportunity for feedback to prevent problems from arising, so risks can be identified earlier, and action taken. The ability to act will not be seen simply through a prism of financial requirements, which can be the case for businesses who work to shareholders. There are different drivers for the organisation. Essentially, co-ops have networks they work with, and those networks offer help and protection.

Reflections

An organisation needs clear leadership, but it also requires effective internal challenge to this leadership. Accepted behaviours and practices can become out of date, and unacceptable to stakeholders, as expectations change and as laws and regulations change. As can be seen from some of the examples provided, this requires constant vigilance. That vigilance is provided by external voices as well – the activists.

The development of appropriate strategies is only as good as the information available to the teams involved and the quality of that team. If it is information-poor or insufficiently resourced, then this increases the level of risk. If the internal challenge is lacking, or not listened to, then similarly, the risks increase. This may be acceptable for a leadership team.

But if a team is uncomfortable with such a stance, then they have little choice but to consider their own position. One tell-tale sign of whether such a leadership team is in place is whether they consider the advice of the Communications department. Does it have a seat at the Board? Are there direct channels to those on the Board? If the answer is no, then that may be a cause for concern.

Along similar lines, governance is considered by some to be the core of ESG because it shapes the actions of the organisation. If the governance of any organisations is lacking, then the E and S may not be considered in a way to address them sufficiently. This may lead, for instance, to company weaknesses not being discussed in reports it issues. If reports only discuss the bright future ahead, they are likely too good to be true. This leaves a trail of breadcrumbs for activists to follow as well. The lower risk option is identifying areas of weakness, and then to map out a path to rectify the situation.

Of course, ESG can be different in different countries. The S may be considered less important in Middle Eastern countries but more important when others are looking at the Middle East. The World Cup in Qatar demonstrated this when these external expectations met the actions of the countries involved. This understanding is important when considering cross-border operations but also when sponsorships and other financial arrangements are made.

This is not to single out the Middle East for failings, especially when it comes to ESG. ESG is not perfectly adhered to around labour rights in many parts of the world. The 2022 ISS ESG reports a rise in workplace discrimination controversies in Australia,[74] and some of their other work does more to highlight variations in ESG trends around the world.[75]

There are a range of constantly shifting expectations which places the onus on companies to maintain a watch not just on what happens in their 'home' countries but also around the world, and not just in relation to themselves. They need to consider the actions of competitors and the attention focused on others by activists.

The emphasis must be on more, rather than less, information being available internally and externally. The idea that poor behaviour can simply be 'washed' away is naïve at best. Some of the worst examples show that the very attempt brings with it more negative attention, making any form of rehabilitation more difficult.

The reaction of some businesses that have found themselves under scrutiny has been to fall back on questionable tactics or communications efforts. Some have tried distraction techniques. But businesses have to consider whether the damage they do to themselves, their operations, their standing and ultimately their reputations is worth it.

Is a better and more beneficial approach to adopt a genuine and transparent approach rather than 'washing' their way out? 'Washing' may be considered a common trend, but is it a sustainable one, and will the divergence between rhetoric and reality eventually catch up with every company that follows it?

Even for those businesses that are moving along a path of genuine commitment and change, public commitments need to match the delivery. The more a gap is allowed to emerge, the more substantial the eventual reputational damage will be. It also gives activists something to aim at.

There are other paths available to business and countries such as engaging positively with activist groups and working with them to find solutions.

Activists will, of course, come with a set of relevant demands, such as a commitment to transparency and progression that can be independently verified, but that may be a price worth agreeing to. Considering the alternative, one dominated by conflict and antagonism, makes collaboration appear increasingly attractive.

In my discussion with Robert Blood, he had advice for companies trying to avoid 'greenwashing':

> Greenwashing is a practice where companies make false or exaggerated claims about the environmental benefits of their products or operations, without actually implementing meaningful sustainability measures. To avoid greenwashing, companies should take the following steps:
>
> 1   Be transparent: Companies should be transparent about their environmental impacts and the steps they are taking to reduce them. This can involve disclosing environmental data, such as greenhouse gas emissions, energy use, and water consumption, and sharing information about their sustainability strategies and goals.
> 2   Provide credible evidence: Companies should provide credible evidence to support their sustainability claims, such as third-party certifications, independent audits, and scientific studies. This can help to build trust and demonstrate that the company is committed to meaningful action.
> 3   Avoid vague or misleading language: Companies should avoid using vague or misleading language in their sustainability communications. This can include terms such as 'eco-friendly', 'sustainable', or 'green', which can be subjective and difficult to verify. Instead, companies should provide specific and measurable information about their sustainability initiatives.
> 4   Focus on real impact: Companies should focus on implementing tangible, measurable sustainability measures that have a real impact on the environment. This can include measures such as reducing greenhouse gas emissions, conserving water, and reducing waste.
> 5   Engage with stakeholders: Companies should engage with stakeholders, such as customers, employees, investors, and NGOs, to gather feedback and ensure that their sustainability initiatives are aligned with stakeholder expectations.
> 6   Continuously improve: Companies should continuously improve their sustainability performance and initiatives, based on feedback and evolving best practices.

Activists appreciate that some businesses respond poorly to scrutiny, but others are prepared to work together on solutions. But they too have constraints and requirements of working with activists. They are not simply going to acquiesce to every demand. A level of understanding and expectation management is required on all parts. But genuine progress can be attained.

Finding ways to work together constructively is always a challenge. Relationships take time to develop. Partnerships require understanding on all parts. An emphasis on pragmatism and being solutions-oriented can deliver progress.

Notes

1 Jesse Coleman 'Leaked: What you should know about Edelman and TransCanada's attack plan', Greenpeace, 20 November 2014, www.greenpeace.org/usa/lea ked-edelman-transcanadas-pr-attack-plan/

2 Jesse Firempong, 'Leaked document details industry's secret plan to defeat Clean Fuel Standard: "Fighting climate change is a losing battle"', Greenpeace, 7 October 2020, www.greenpeace.org/canada/en/press-release/43575/leaked-docum ent-details-industrys-secret-plan-to-defeat-clean-fuel-standard-fighting-climate-chan ge-is-a-losing-battle/

3 See Ben Martin, 'HSBC pledges to stop funding new oil and gasfields', *The Times*, 15 December 2022, www.thetimes.co.uk/article/hsbc-pledges-to-stop-fun ding-new-oil-and-gasfields-2kszb9g20

4 Competitions and Markets Authority, 'CMA to scrutinise "green" claims in sales of household essentials', press release, 26 January 2023, www.gov.uk/governm ent/news/cma-to-scrutinise-green-claims-in-sales-of-household-essentials

5 Competitions and Markets Authority, 'CMA to scrutinise "green" claims in sales of household essentials', press release, 26 January 2023, www.gov.uk/governm ent/news/cma-to-scrutinise-green-claims-in-sales-of-household-essentials

6 Competition and Markets Authority, 'ASOS, Boohoo and Asda: Greenwashing investigation', cases and projects, 26 January 2023, www.gov.uk/cma-cases/asos-boohoo-and-asda-greenwashing-investigation#compliance-review

7 Competition and Markets Authority, 'ASOS, Boohoo and Asda: Greenwashing investigation', 26 January 2023, www.gov.uk/cma-cases/asos-boohoo-and-asda -greenwashing-investigation#compliance-review

8 Competition and Markets Authority, 'Making environmental claims on goods and services', guidance, 20 September 2021, www.gov.uk/government/publica tions/green-claims-code-making-environmental-claims/environmental-claims-on -goods-and-services

9 Competition and Markets Authority, 'Global sweep finds 40% of firms' green claims could be misleading', press release, 28 January 2021, www.gov.uk/gov ernment/news/global-sweep-finds-40-of-firms-green-claims-could-be-misleading

10 Financial Conduct Authority, 'FCA proposes new rules to tackle greenwashing', press release, 25 October 2022, www.fca.org.uk/news/press-releases/fca-prop oses-new-rules-tackle-greenwashing

11 Ellen Ormesher, '8 times brands fell foul of ASA for "greenwashing"', *The Drum*, 23 March 2022, www.thedrum.com/news/2022/03/23/8-times-brands-fell-foul-asa-greenwashing

12 Mei Li, Gregory Trencher and Iusen Asuka, 'The clean energy claims of BP, Chevron, ExxonMobil and Shell: A mismatch between discourse, actions and investments', *Plos One*, 16 February 2022, https://journals.plos.org/plosone/a rticle?id=10.1371/journal.pone.0263596

13 James Wright, 'Letter: CIPR: "Greenwash" is now everywhere', *PR Week*, 24 April 2008, www.prweek.com/article/804619/letter-cipr-greenwash-everywhere

14 PRCA, 'Comms industry must be brave and embrace leadership role in fight for climate truth – PRCA research', press release, 7 July 2022, https://newsroom. prca.org.uk/pressreleases/comms-industry-must-be-brave-and-embrace-leadership -role-in-fight-for-climate-truth-prca-research-3193812

15 PRCA, 'Hit play – climate communication group launches with a focus on collaboration and education', press release, 6 March 2023, https://newsroom.prca. org.uk/pressreleases/hit-play-climate-communication-group-launches-with-a-focu s-on-collaboration-and-education-3237602

16 Open Democracy, 'PR firm accused of greenwashing big oil is helping organise COP27', press release, 21 October 2022, www.opendemocracy.net/en/cop27-hill knowlton-pr-greenwash-egypt/

17 António Guterres, 'Secretary-General's address to the General Assembly', United Nations, 20 September 2022, www.un.org/sg/en/content/sg/speeches/2022-09-20/ secretary-generals-address-the-general-assembly

18 United Nations, 'Integrity matters: Net zero commitments by business, financial institutions, cities and regions: United Nations' High-Level Expert Group on the net zero emissions commitments of non-state entities', November 2022, www.un. org/sites/un2.un.org/files/high-level_expert_group_n7b.pdf

19 United Nations, '"Zero tolerance for greenwashing", Guterres says at report launch', press release, 10 November 2022, www.un.org/en/delegate/'zero-tolera nce-greenwashing'-guterres-says-report-launch

20 Clean Creatives, 'Clean Creatives issues "THE F-LIST 2021" report detailing 90 ad and PR companies working for the fossil fuel industry', press release, 21 September 2021,   https://cleancreatives.org/news/clean-creatives-issues-the-f-list-2021-report-detailing-90-ad-and-pr-companies-working-for-the-fossil-fuel-industry

21 Influence Map, 'US heavy-duty transport & climate change', December 2022, https:// influencemap.org/report/US-Heavy-Duty-Transport-Climate-Change-20434

22 House of Representatives, 'Committee on oversight and reform, memorandum', 9 December 2022, www.documentcloud.org/documents/23560709-2022-12-09-cor-supplemental-memo-fossil-fuel-industry-disinformation

23 Catherine Clifford, 'Democratic lawmakers accuse big oil companies of "greenwashing"', CNBC, 9 December 2022, www.cnbc.com/2022/12/09/democratic-la wmakers-accuse-big-oil-of-greenwashing.html; see also NBC, 'House committee claims oil companies could "doom" climate', 10 December 2022, www.youtube. com/watch?v=sFhSDwrrM_Q

24 Stefano Gelmini, 'We're living in a golden age of greenwash', Greenpeace blog, 29 June 2021, www.greenpeace.org.uk/news/golden-age-of-greenwash/

25 Climate Change Committee, 'The role of transition plans in the UK's pathway to net zero', 26 May 2022, www.theccc.org.uk/publication/the-role-of-transition-pla ns-in-the-uks-pathway-to-net-zero-ricardo-energy-environment/

26 Climate Change Committee, 'The role of transition plans in the UK's pathway to net zero', 26 May 2022, www.theccc.org.uk/publication/the-role-of-transition-pla ns-in-the-uks-pathway-to-net-zero-ricardo-energy-environment/

27 Competition and Markets Authority, 'ASOS, Boohoo and ASDA: Greenwashing investigation', cases and projects, 26 January 2023, www.gov.uk/cma-cases/asos-boohoo-and-asda-greenwashing-investigation

28 Such as an undercover investigation by The Times. See Tom Ball, 'My month undercover at BooHoo: "A wrist strap tracks our every move"', The Times, 22 November 2022, www.thetimes.com/uk/article/boohoo-warehouse-shift-investigation-80z2fq0qj

29 RSA, 'Fast fashion's plastic problem: Sustainability and material usage in online fashion', Briefing 010, 11 June 2021, www.thersa.org/globalassets/reports/2021/fa st-fashions-plastic-problem.pdf

30 Niloufar Haidari, 'Kourtney Kardashian wants to make BooHoo's fast-fashion sustainable. Spoiler alert: She can't', *The Guardian*, 12 September 2022, www.theguardian.com/fashion/2022/sep/12/kourtney-kardashian-boohoo-fast-fashion-sustainable

31 Competition and Markets Authority, *Green Claims Code*, 16 September 2021, https://youtu.be/kCArp_mCtfI

32 HM Treasury, 'New independent group to help tackle "greenwashing"', news story, 9 June 2021, www.gov.uk/government/news/new-independent-group-to-help-tackle-greenwashing

33 Stephanie Ebbs and Elizabeth Schulze, 'Biden administration faces increasing calls to stop companies from "greenwashing"', *ABC News*, 8 April 2021, https://abcnews.go.com/Politics/biden-administration-faces-increasing-calls-stop-companies-greenwashing/story?id=76907048

34 US Securities and Exchange Commission, 'SEC announces enforcement task force focused on climate and ESG issues', press release, 4 March 2021, www.sec.gov/news/press-release/2021-42

35 BlackRock, 'Larry Fink's 2021 letter to CEOs', www.blackrock.com/us/individual/2021-larry-fink-ceo-letter

36 BlackRock, 'Larry Fink's 2021 letter to CEOs', www.blackrock.com/us/individual/2021-larry-fink-ceo-letter

37 BlackRock, 'Larry Fink's 2022 letter to CEOs', www.blackrock.com/corporate/investor-relations/larry-fink-ceo-letter

38 HSBC, *Annual Reports and Account 2022, ESG Review*, 070 (see www.hsbc.com/who-we-are/esg-and-responsible-business/esg-reporting-centre)

39 Kalyeena Makortoff, 'HSBC suspends head of responsible investing who called climate warnings "shrill"', *The Guardian*, 22 May 2022, www.theguardian.com/business/2022/may/22/hsbc-suspends-head-of-responsible-investing-who-called-climate-warnings-shrill

40 Stuart Kirk, LinkedIn post, www.linkedin.com/posts/stuart-kirk-267551b6_today-i-wish-to-announce-that-i-have-resigned-activity-6950772878405459968-XWcJ/

41 Lawyers for Climate Action, 'Advertising Standards Board rules "zero carbon gas" advertising campaign is misleading', 22 July 2021, www.lawyersforclimateaction.nz/news-events/firstgas-decision

42 OECD, 'National Contact Points for the OECD guidelines for multinational enterprises', 9 December 2016, https://web-archive.oecd.org/2016-12-09/82328-ncps.htm

43 OECD, 'Annual report on the OECD guidelines for multinational enterprises 2020', 2021, http://mneguidelines.oecd.org/2020-Annual-Report-MNE-Guidelines-EN.pdf

44 OECD, 'Providing access to remedy: 20 years and the road ahead', 2020, https://mneguidelines.oecd.org/NCPs-for-RBC-providing-access-to-remedy-20-years-and-the-road-ahead.pdf

45 For a helpful explainer see Carolina Descio, 'The EU taxonomy explained: Here's what it means for financial services', Carbon Trust Insights, 22 September 2022, www.carbontrust.com/news-and-insights/insights/the-eu-taxonomy-explained-heres-what-it-means-for-financial-services

46 See Brandalism's Twitter / X account, https://twitter.com/BrandalismUK/status/1614895234667741185?s=20&t=4x-381NXBqUrbBYxIWEYMA

47 For a background piece on the organisation see Harriet Sherwood, 'Led By Donkeys show their faces at last: "No one knew it was us"', *The Guardian*, 25 May 2019 www.theguardian.com/politics/2019/may/25/led-by-donkeys-reveal-identities-brexit-billboards-posters

48 See www.instagram.com/ledbydonkeys

49 South Pole, 'Going green, then going dark – one in four companies are keeping quiet on science-based targets', press release, 18 October 2022, www.southpole.com/news/going-green-then-going-dark

50 Planet Tracker, 'The greenwashing hydra', January 2023, https://planet-tracker.org/wp-content/uploads/2023/01/Greenwashing-Hydra-3.pdf

51 Sensu, '50 shades of greenwashing research report: How to create effective ESG communications', 2 January 2023, https://sensuinsight.com/50-shades-of-greenwashing-research-report-how-to-create-effective-esg-communications/?utm_source=substack&utm_medium=email

52 Andrew Edgecliffe-Johnson, 'Mars chief hits out at "nonsense" attacks on corporate ESG', *Financial Times*, 19 March 2023, www.ft.com/content/15ba3866-b444-4c7a-bb6c-7f187b84be07

53 Tessa Wernink, 'What if we get it right: Activists and innovators, Part 2. Employee activism: Change from within', podcast, 10 May 2023, www.whatifwegetitright.com/season-3-episodes/employee-activism-change-from-within

54 KPMG, 'Climate quitting – younger workers voting with their feet on employer's ESG commitments', press release, 24 January 2023, https://kpmg.com/uk/en/home/media/press-releases/2023/01/climate-quitting-younger-workers-voting-esg.html

55 Discussed on Neville Hobson and Shel Holtz, 'For immediate release: Employees caught in activism's crossfire', 343, 20 July 2023, www.firpodcastnetwork.com/fir-343-employees-caught-in-activisms-crossfire/

56 See www.livgolf.com

57 United Nations Human Rights, 'Khashoggi killing: UN human rights expert says Saudi Arabia is responsible for "premeditated execution"', press release, 19 June 2019, www.ohchr.org/en/press-releases/2019/06/khashoggi-killing-un-human-rights-expert-says-saudi-arabia-responsible

58 United Nations Human Rights, 'Khashoggi killing: UN human rights expert says Saudi Arabia is responsible for "premeditated execution"', press release, 19 June 2019, www.ohchr.org/en/press-releases/2019/06/khashoggi-killing-un-human-rights-expert-says-saudi-arabia-responsible

59 David Mercer, 'Why LIV Golf is the most controversial tournament in sport right now', *Sky News*, 9 June 2022, https://news.sky.com/story/why-liv-golf-is-the-most-controversial-tournament-in-sport-right-now-12629948

60 For an exploration of the criticisms made of Edelman see Adam Lowenstein, 'The world's biggest PR firm claims to be an expert on trust – but is it?', *The Guardian*, 15 January 2023, www.theguardian.com/business/2023/jan/15/edelman-pr-firm-davos-trust

61 It also requires consideration of governance arrangements both formal and informal, see Frederik Dahlmann and Wendy Stubbs, 'Purpose framing as an informal governance approach to sustainability transformations in the private sector', *Earth System Governance*, 15 (January 2023), www.sciencedirect.com/science/article/pii/S2589811623000022

62 Arun Sudhaman '"This is smart business, not woke delusion": Edelman defends brand activism', *PRovoke Media*, 18 January 2023, www.provokemedia.com/latest/article/this-is-smart-business-not-woke-delusion-edelman-defends-brand-activism

63 Glasgow Financial Alliance For Net Zero, www.gfanzero.com

64 Steerpike, 'British universities took £24 million from China', *The Spectator*, 25 April 2022, www.spectator.co.uk/article/british-universities-took-24-million-from-china/

65 Geraldine Scott, 'Universities have 'risky' ties to China', *The Times*, 22 January 2023, www.thetimes.co.uk/article/universities-have-risky-ties-to-china-h5cjtw05q

66 Will Crisp, 'Natural History Museum under fire for gagging clause with Danish oil sponsor', *The Guardian*, 8 January 2023, www.theguardian.com/culture/2023/jan/08/natural-history-museum-gagging-order-danish-oil-sponsor

67 See https://fossilfreelondon.org

68 See Hypebae, 'Employee calls out Adidas for silence regarding Ye's antisemitic tweets', 25 October 2022, https://hypebae.com/2022/10/adidas-director-calls-out-company-kanye-west-tweets-latest-info; and Hypebae, 'An Adidas director calls out company for remaining silent about Ye's anti-semitism', 25 October 2022, https://hypebeast.com/2022/10/adidas-director-calls-out-company-silent-about-kanye-west-anti-semitism-info

69 See Jaclyn Peiser and Jacob Bogage, 'Kanye West's antisemitism cost him Adidas and most of his empire', *Washington Post*, 25 October 2022, www.washingtonpost.com/business/2022/10/25/adidas-kanye-west-partnership-ends/; and Jordan Hoffman, 'Pressure mounts on Adidas to cut ties with Kanye West', *Vanity Fair*, 22 October 2022 www.vanityfair.com/style/2022/10/pressure-mounts-on-adidas-to-cut-ties-with-kanye-west

70 Clean Clothes Campaign, 'Activists' high-profile hoax highlights Adidas' hypocrisy', 15 January 2023, https://cleanclothes.org/news/2023/activists-high-profile-hoax-highlights-adidas-hypocrisy?utm_source=substack&utm_medium=email

71 If you are interested in knowing more about the campaign then you can read Coop, 'Safer colleagues, safer communities', November 2018, https://assets.ctfassets.net/5ywmq66472jr/5gVLAxiM5ikCC8qeOKwIUG/97489631d2e8eee6d07ce152369f81f9/Safer_Colleagues_Safer_Communities_Nov_2018.pdf; and the follow-up Coop, 'Safer colleagues, safer communities: One year on', 2020, https://downloads.ctfassets.net/5ywmq66472jr/2JBAfUJvV66vbMejr9kHKY/8cce1a59e34904a19c83069edc49181b/safer-colleagues-safer-communities-one-year-on.pdf

72 You can read the full report at Coop, '"It's not part of the job": Violence and verbal abuse towards shop workers: A review of evidence and policy', September 2019, https://assets.ctfassets.net/5ywmq66472jr/22QfMejeWYbimJ9ykX9W9h/0e99f15c0ed24c16ab74d38b42d5129a/It_s_not_part_of_the_job_report.pdf

73 You can read the full report at Coop, 'Breaking the cycle: gaining the views of criminal justice practitioners and retail offenders on effective sentencing', May 2021, https://assets.ctfassets.net/5ywmq66472jr/12VK4Uvg808UkGUAaB0gXG/53d06cb910321bf2ff35bd18acb52d5a/Breaking_the_Cycle_report_final.pdf

74 ISS ESG, 'Corporate controversies that defined 2022', 14 December 2022, www.issgovernance.com/library/corporate-controversies-that-defined-2022/

75 ISS ESG, 'ISS ESG 2023 report identifies key 2023 regional ESG opportunities and risks for investors', press release, 23 March 2023, https://insights.issgovernance.com/posts/iss-esg-2023-report-identifies-key-2023-regional-esg-opportunities-and-risks-for-investors/#:~:text=Key%20takeaways%20from%20ISS%20ESG%27s,concerns%20that%20cut%20across%20regions

Conclusion

Learning lessons

Activism is a part of a vibrant civil society and no organisation should consider itself immune from scrutiny. But activism is constantly broadening its scope and, particularly in the case of climate change, its appeal.

But that scope also means the tactics constantly broaden and evolve. The targets too are broader but with a forensic focus on the aim of the campaign. That means that many organisations need to be more aware of the likelihood of being the subject of an activist campaign.

For many companies, gone are the days of confrontation because they know the impact that reputational damage can have. They also cannot 'PR' their way out of a problem. Activists have become increasingly adept at maintaining a focus over a period of time or, at the very least, returning to the issue to ensure that any promised change was genuine. Any initial response from a company, even if it takes the heat out of the problem early on, is only the starting point. You cannot make the problem simply 'go away'.

This is in part due to activists no longer simply being a small and dedicated group of motivated individuals. There is a core that will always be more motivated, but what activists have been very successful in doing is using changing technology to provide individuals with low/zero cost options which take very little time to deploy. Initially such people were called 'clickivists', but over time such action has been shown to be highly effective, not least in highlighting causes with the media. The sheer weight of numbers can sometimes prove highly effective.

The issue of the use of technology was fully illustrated by Direct Action Everywhere (DxE) when it released its Investigation Manual that they consider 'breaks down the best practices for executing investigations and exposing animal cruelty'.[1] The release of the 150-page manual was focused on encouraging others to join the DxE's mission. But Lewis Bernier, a long-time investigator at DxE, speaking to *Wired*, suggested that it was 'an acknowledgement that groups around the world, from Europe to Australia to South America, are already carrying out investigations similar to DxE's. He says the guide is an attempt to create an information hub across those groups'.[2]

DOI: 10.4324/9781003371908-7

The manual considers everything from security and cybersecurity through to biosecurity protocols. It also explains the role that spy cams, night vision and drones can play.

Technology for activists is not simply about the internet or social media, but many others now more readily and cheaply available. Another factor is that it does not require specialist knowledge to operate. This opens up not just the opportunities for activism but also the numbers able to take part.

Thanks to the role of various technologies, knowledge and evidence can be more easily obtained and shared. Keeping the pressure up also undermines some of the ways in which businesses and countries have tried to deflect attention, 'washing' their reputations with the public and other stakeholders.

Activists using brands

As the WE Communications report, 'Healthy reputation: More than medicine', shows, activists can use an organisation's brand to hold the company to account.[3] It could be argued in a way that governments, passing new laws and regulations, can be slow, but activists can move quickly to place a spotlight on problems; they can also be more aggressive, more creative and more purposefully damaging in their approach.

For the authors of the report, it is clear that 'corporate brand matters – a lot'.[4] 'Our findings show that HCPs (healthcare professionals) worldwide want the peace of mind that they are prescribing treatments from brands they respect. Building that respect goes well beyond producing high-quality drug therapies'.[5]

According to the report, corporate reputation is the No1 factor that influences a decision to prescribe and, on the flip side, there would be a reluctance to prescribe or recommend a medication by a company with a poor reputation.

We can see why in this sector, and doubtless others, the fight for reputations is so critical. Knowing and appreciating that is valuable knowledge for activists.

But it also highlights the apparent immediacy of activism. In a way that government action can be a long time in coming, and some may choose not to change their behaviour until forced to, activism applies heat to a situation immediately. Organisations that are unaware of that, or choose to ignore it, are running increased risks.

Some governments may actually be happy with this approach as it removes the responsibility from them and means there is less onus on them to pass new laws. In the end they may still have to pass laws but only to deal with the more extreme examples of poor behaviour which in itself provides some justification.

Governments are generally reticent to pass new laws. They take time, use up valuable political capital and may not be popular within all sections of their own parties. So instead, government and activists can try to see how powerful existing laws are in campaigns to change behaviour and ensure that action is taken.

Even if new laws are not passed, activists have been adept at utilising laws that are already on the statute books. The way that Shell is being held to account under Company Law shows what activists are trying to do.

That creativity, guile and focus on outcomes could only be dreamed of in many corporate settings. Whether this comes from a lack of resources, or low levels of motivation and dedication, or all thee, is unclear. It is simply the case that those on the receiving end of an activist campaign have to be prepared for that.

It may be that different parts of a business could have different views of activists. This lack of unity could stifle or undermine a coherent response.

Fundamentally, we are looking at a policy vs performance issue. Either policies are not in place so delivery does not happen, or the policies are in place and they are not delivered on. In either scenario, an audience will eventually call that out.

Performance can also be measured against competitors. Ground lost against competitors in an area of activist concern allows a potentially ever-expanding gap to emerge. That increases the expose to activist action and in the meantime customers are lost and reputations damaged.

Divergences and similarities

Many have too simplistic a view of activists. They see them as detrimental to the operation of an organisation. The reality is more complex and nuanced.

There are activist governments, activist regulators, activist consumers, activist charities, activist brands and so on. It would be impossible to list them all. Each 'type' of activist will have their own motivations and methods of engagement, but each rightly requires a response.

It remains clear that many organisations – businesses and activists – do not really understand each other. Some organisations may welcome tighter regulations or new laws that restrict activist actions, in whatever arena they arise in, but that massively underestimates an activists' commitment to the cause. Blocking one type of action only means it reinvents itself as another form of action.

It would help if more organisations appreciated the challenges that face activists.

These often include:

- Restrictions on activities – some activists face censorship or surveillance, or their ability to organise or undertake some forms of activity are restricted. Some will simply break the law or others will look for new, often creative, ways to be active. Restrictions do not make the issues go away.

- Resources – there is a constant need for activists to look for funds but also people.
- Personal impacts – activists can struggle to cope with the personal demands of their activism. Not least, some put themselves in harm's way or are liable to be arrested and imprisoned.
- Time – their struggle can take a long time to bear fruit and it can seem like a never-ending challenge. Whereas individuals and teams in businesses move around, there is a longevity to activism, if that is what is needed.

Despite these types of challenges, activists continue to push for change. That sheer motivation, conviction and commitment are often massively underestimated by businesses.

But businesses also fail to consider:

- The long-term impact of activist action – it is often thought about in the narrow sense of what it means for them in the here and now.
- How activism will continue to develop – they do not always consider how the challenge may evolve in future and the forms it could take.
- How technology continues to provide more options and will be utilised in future.
- Traditional sledgehammers will not work – simply relying on expensive legal action or 'response' communications campaigns is not only ineffective but can actually be a spur to activists.

In this era, there is simply no excuse for not paying attention to what activists are doing. No company or government should find anything a surprise. This monitoring of activist activity should be a base.

There is a wide range of ways to keep up-to-date with activist activity:

- Follow relevant activist organisations – those relevant to the business or who are active in campaigns focused on competitors. They often publish reports, newsletters and press releases that provide updates on their campaigns and activities.
- Social media channels – follow them and see what updates they share.
- News media – many newspapers and broadcasters carry coverage on activism and social justice issues.
- Attend events – especially those organised by activist groups so that you can hear directly from leaders, members, experts and others.
- Engage directly – there are many ways in which outreach can happen – in-person and online. The concept of a genuine dialogue where questions can be asked, knowledge exchanged and support offered not only enhances understanding of an issue but the challenges faced by a range of stakeholders.

Whilst my initial emphasis was on keeping up-to-date with activist activity, the same approach works perfectly for activists keeping up-to-date with business or government activity as well. The reality is that the challenges faced by activists and businesses alike are not that different from one another:

- Communications – at the heart of campaigns and responses to campaigns.
- Funding – required and often limited.
- The role of politics – it plays a critical role for both and government is a key audience for both.
- The development of partnerships – the realisation that a partnership approach can be an effective way forward.
- Friends and allies – the broader and deeper a network the more robust a campaign or response will be.

Collaboration

There are an increasing number of examples of activists and businesses working together to drive change. Some examples include:

- Patagonia connecting with environmental groups through its Action Works.
- Ben and Jerry's social justice activism working with organisations such as Close the Workhouse, a campaign against a St Louis jail.
- The Body Shop's human rights activism such as its partnership with Plan UK to fight for equality for girls and young women.
- Bank of America's LGBTQIA+ activism and efforts to promote diversity which includes partnerships with Black Enterprise, Out & Equal and The Hispanic Promise, amongst many others.

However, the reality is that such partnerships do not always work well. There is often no one reason why it does not work out, but this could include everything from a lack of resources or commitment (on either part) to a poor choice of partner. Having a partnership in place does not mean that failures cannot happen. Shell has long partnered with environmental organisations but environmental failures still happen. Nike's partnerships with labour organisations do not mean it does not come under fire around the alleged use of forced labour or the low payment offered to workers.

In many cases, there may be ongoing criticism, but most companies have changed and improved their practices.

Partnering with an activist group can help a business find its way out of a problem. The expertise of the group can help to develop and implement practical solutions. In addition, there is no harm in having really committed individuals knowing that a business is trying and continues to try to solve the issue. However, this will not make criticism go away. Across many issues it may be possible to work with one set of activists but continue to face criticism from other, potentially more radical, groups.

When Nike faced criticism over its approach to labour rights, it worked with groups to develop codes of conduct and improve transparency. Activists continue to maintain and look for, for example, the effective and consistent enforcement of codes.

Commitment always needs to be matched by delivery and also an appreciation that expectations will continue to increase.

What makes for a good collaborative relationship?

The ground rules need to be set out in some form of agreement or Memorandum of Understanding to build trust from the outset. That will need to cover matters such as:

- transparency and sharing of materials
- real input into decision-making with appropriate governance arrangements
- respected individuals who will take part
- funding as there may be a disparity which could limit input
- timings and especially how long any initial agreement is for; it needs to be long enough to build trust.

Even the most constructive of partnerships will not make issues simply go away. Commitment is required on both parts.

Just as activists face choices about whether to work with a business, so does the business. Considerations will include:

- Unity of activists – activists are not always united. Some may see collaboration as a betrayal, so bringing some activists into the decision-making process will necessarily end a campaign.
- Unity of a business – similarly, there may not be unity within a business either. Some may view collaboration as a failure of leadership or of 'giving in' to a campaign.
- Impact on the opposition – working together could embolden those groups not chosen to become an 'insider' group. The 'outsiders' may become even more active.
- Selection of partners – this applies equally to an activist group or a business – how to decide who to work with? Relevant considerations will include:

    a   personal relationships and trust
    b   previous engagement

c   consideration of whether the values and the aims of the organisation align
d   how the collaboration will be explained
e   the commitment to change
f   the finance allocated and timescales attached
g   the length of time allocated for the work
h   the reaction of stakeholders and other bodies
i   agreement about how challenges will be overcome during the period of the collaboration
j   agreement over measures of success, how these will be reviewed and evaluated
k   the potential for a continued relationship if deemed successful by all parties.

Businesses should not consider working with activists simply as a means of avoiding reputational damage. If real change is not delivered then there will be an inevitable backlash causing even greater reputational damage, with all the associated consequences.

The mindset also needs to shift from addressing issues to getting ahead of issues. Too much activity is focused on problems that have already been encountered rather than anticipating challenges and working with activists in that.

The critical issue is how companies and governments can get ahead of the issues. Working in a collegiate way with activist groups should not be viewed as a sign of weakness, as some may consider it. It is not about giving in but actually about working together to solve an issue that could otherwise fester and get worse over time.

The reality is that activists shine a light on an issue that will, at some stage, need to be addressed. There is a choice about how and when to address the challenge, but it will, at some stage, need to be addressed.

If organisations fail to appreciate this then they are failing both in their responsibilities to shareholders and in taking steps to understand what their purpose is outside of making returns for shareholders.

No organisation should ever assume they know what an activist is, what they do or how they behave. This only happens through engagement, because each relationship between an activist and an organisation is unique.

Speaking to Sarah Waddington CBE, an activist and communicator, about the relationship between activists and businesses, we discussed why any organisation should consider social issues as a key driver for them:

> Social issues are linked to sustainability and legacy. What kind of company do you want to be and what kind of world do you want to leave behind?

Today's talent chooses to work for organisations committed to delivering impact in the least damaging way, and ideally in a way that leaves society in a better place.

The same goes for consumers when they choose who to buy from, and increasingly for asset managers and financiers when they're looking where to invest.

If that's not an incentive to smarten up working practices, I don't know what is.

In which case, how can any organisation best demonstrate that they are socially driven?

Organisations that are truly socially driven focus inwards rather than on performative action. They invest in insight, innovation and longer-term outcomes.

This means bypassing the first and most obvious solutions and finding those which might be harder and more costly to achieve, but have more impact. Offsetting is a great example of this and often management teams will tick this box and stop there when the results are negligible.

Even when steps are taken, an organisation can find itself on the receiving end of a campaign / activist activity. Under those circumstances, Sarah looked to Vanilla Ice for inspiration.

Vanilla Ice might seem an unlikely go to here but 'Stop, collaborate and listen' is pretty good advice in this situation. Stakeholder engagement is crucial and never more than when you're moving into potential crisis management territory.

Good practice is to monitor and engage with stakeholders based on the power and interest / influence they hold. The key is to do this authentically and follow through with changes where they're required in an appropriate timeframe.

But there are, she suggests, some fundamental misunderstandings that you have experienced between businesses and activists.

The irony of social media is that it has created anti-social behaviours in which organisations and individuals broadcast their views rather than communicate by listening to each other's perspectives. It becomes about who can shout loudest and then who has the deepest pockets for promotion.

Activists don't always appreciate the political, legal and economic constrictions and parameters that organisations work within. Equally, directors aren't always open-minded enough to alternate views and other ways of operating, which might require financing that impacts short-term goals.

Two-way education that leads to agreement or compromise is important, as well as acknowledgement that even small changes in the right direction equal progress. That gets lost far too often.

We discussed how established businesses, especially large ones, can 'retrofit' themselves to become more socially driven and aware – Sarah forcefully challenged this assumption.

If you're an established business, please do not waste time retrofitting what you do.

Instead, take stock of the world around you, understand the principles and imperatives that come with being a socially driven business and start to have the challenging conversations that are created by revisiting your organisational purpose with a view to the future.

It can feel overwhelming, so a good starting point is breaking activity down so that it can be measured across different criteria. Distributing responsibility across the organisation and aiming for incremental progress rather than overnight change can also improve the chances of success.

New era

For too long, existing 'definitions' have led to confrontation. Activists are typically seen in a negative light by businesses, and other audiences, with their activities doing little other than imposing costs. But it is a more nuanced reality. There are different types of groups, different actions and different supporters.

Activism is in the eye of the beholder – that brings with it assumptions, often personal, which can easily distract from a fair assessment of the cause. It therefore also impacts on the response.

A constructive relationship can be developed only if an understanding is developed. How do you strike up any sort of relationship if there is little understanding on either part?

Leaders can be detached from activist issues in an optimism bubble. The more senior a leader, the more likely it is that they will overestimate the degree of approachability and their listening skills. This can mean they underestimate the strength of feeling felt by their audience, including employees. There is work to be done in finding out what matters. Assumptions may not, as Jack Reacher suggests, kill, but they can do serious reputational damage.

As much as a 'say-do' gap can deliver problems, gaps in understanding and perspective can increase reputational and operational risks. The modern reality is that no organisation can sit on the activism fence. Inaction is as political as action. An organisation needs to make authentic choices about what to get involved in and what not to get involved in. Each requires an active and present decision. That decision needs to be documented. Audiences will be looking to understand decisions.

Activists, of course, need stunts to bring attention to their campaigns. But there is also the danger that some groups enter into active competition with one another. Was Greenpeace scaling the UK Prime Minister's house maintaining pressure on the government and / or a fight to be taken seriously again having been out campaigned by Just Stop Oil?

Governments and businesses should be proud to have an active activist community. This scrutiny can make them behave like a better organisation. They bring to light issues that you may not have sight of and can help work through solutions, but only if engaged with.

Activists lead today where companies tread tomorrow. They motivate supporters over time. They build knowledge and credibility. The reality of modern-day reputations built and defended under the glare of social media means constant scrutiny. That, combined with creative activists, maintains pressure. The activism is both internal and external, but both working hard to maintain that scrutiny in a very public way. Activists know and understand the importance of reputation. That is the new reality.

The reality of trying to 'wash' your way out of real change or using it to slow the process of change does little to achieve either aim. As has been discussed, 'washing' may be popular but that does not make challenges go away. That is not to say that communication cannot play a positive role in explaining when changes and improvements have been made but it is not a substitute for change.

What steps should activists take? The simplest and most effective one is to continue to appreciate the value of a target's reputation and apply pressure on it. That is something that leadership teams understand, and it can elicit a prompt response.

What steps should organisational and business leaders take?

- Watch and listen – externally, this means paying attention to the sector, to competitors and the latest activist actions; internally, it includes dialogue as well. There needs to be constant vigilance.
- Build engagement – across stakeholder audiences, internally and externally.
- Emphasise long-term relationships – actions should be about building for the long term rather than potentially a series of short-term hits.
- Deliver what is promised – never allow the 'say-do' gap to grow.

A response to activism will always have consequences. What do stakeholders such as employees think of what has happened? Many organisational leaders think that their response is the last action but that is far from the case. The response from leaders can take different forms. From ignoring an activists' actions through to 'washing' and then on to defensive engagement, often legally led because they feel forced to, and then on to those that make a step change in the culture of an organisation.

On the Masters of Scale podcast, Priya Parker, author of *The Art of Gathering*,[6] discussed hybrid working. The points made can, I believe, can be applied to working with outside groups, such as activists, as well as inside groups – consider who talks, respect their time, and learn the skill of gathering.

Delivery is fundamental to any organisation. Whether that is a business, charity, or government. But getting to the delivery endpoint is part of the story. No one expects an organisation to get to the proposed endpoint in one go. That has to be part of the story. Businesses should not shy away from that.

There is then a choice for the organisation. Do they go silent during the journey to the endpoint or do they provide information throughout. There can be an assumption that the release of the information has to be loud and in public. That is not always the case. Instead, updating key audiences may be sufficient.

All organisations need to consider:

- power and empowerment
- how decisions are made
- what public statements and commitments are arrived at.

Activists can either be empowered or will look for ways to empower themselves.

Genuine action is always needed but even that will not make a problem go away. The spotlight might move away for a while as the behaviour and actions of others are scrutinised, but it will return to ensure that commitments made have been delivered. As others improve their behaviour and actions, activists will look to secure further improvements. If there is a deviation from a previous commitment or a failure to deliver, that brings the spotlight back even sooner. There is nothing worse than the failure to deliver on a promise.

Growing activism

All the indicators are that activism will continue to grow in strength and importance. Employee activism will be a defining feature of the workplace. Organisational leadership can itself, as we have seen, be activism. The law is a tool. Evolving technology is an enabler.

An organisation that puts its head in the sand is asking for trouble. A lack of information from them now seems to facilitate deep fakes, conspiracy theories and challenge without pushback. When a vacuum or even a temporary void exists, it will be filled by the commentary and speculation of others. It could be all the incentive needed for a campaign to take hold.

Having no position may be thought to prevent some challenges, like a political attack, but this only leaves space for others, such as activists. Activists can be right to challenge because it forces the company to come out into the spotlight with a stance on the matter. Why should executives be the ones to make such decisions? Surely other stakeholders, not least employees, should be involved? That is certainly the direction of travel of expectations.

It is a similar situation when it comes to government engagement. Some businesses seem rather scared of political interaction and leave to make the decisions without hindrance. However, rather than waiting for, for instance, standards or regulations to be written, why should not companies help to write them and work with others to do so? Activists push for this. They see the value in it.

High standards must be maintained and subsequently further enhanced whether governments choose to get involved or not. There is no actual endpoint. Businesses need to come to terms with that reality. Activists will always keep pushing.

We moved beyond PR some time ago, but not everyone appreciates that yet.

Notes

1 Direct Action Everywhere, 'How to expose animal abuse', 7 November 2023, www.directactioneverywhere.com/theliberationist/investigation-manual?utm_campaign=dxe-io-manual&utm_medium=shortlink&utm_source=dxe-io
2 Andy Greenberg, 'This is the ops manual for the most tech-savvy animal liberation group in the US', Wired, 8 November 2023, www.wired.com/story/dxe-animal-agriculture-investigation-guide
3 WE Brands in Motion, 'Healthy reputation: More than medicine', 2023 www.we-worldwide.com/media/452450/we-brands-in-motion-2023_healthy-reputation.pdf
4 WE Brands in Motion, 'Healthy reputation: More than medicine', 2023, p. 1, www.we-worldwide.com/media/452450/we-brands-in-motion-2023_healthy-reputation.pdf
5 WE Brands in Motion, 'Healthy reputation: More than medicine', 2023, p. 1, www.we-worldwide.com/media/452450/we-brands-in-motion-2023_healthy-reputation.pdf
6 Masters of Scale podcast, 6 October 2022, 'Mastering the hybrid workplace', with Priya Parker, https://mastersofscale.com/mastering-the-hybrid-workplace-priya-parker

Index

Bold page numbers indicate figures, *italic* numbers indicate tables.

Printed in the United States
by Baker & Taylor Publisher Services